BREATH

The Light No Stars Are Made Of - 2000
Oh Cabezon - 2001
Breath - 2002
Poems

LARRY GOODELL

©2021 by Larry Goodell
All Rights Reserved

ACKNOWLEDGMENTS
"Easter Sunday 2000" and "Anthrax Avenue" appeared in *the Malpais Review,* Summer 2012.
"Alien Classified" first appeared in *Unlikely Stories,* Episode IV.

BY THE POET
Escape - poems 2003-2007; *Grounded* - poems 2008-2010;
Commons - poems 2017-2019 duende press 2020.
Nothing To Laugh About - poems 2015-2016 Beatlick Press 2018.
Pieces of Heart - poems of 2014 Beatlick Press 2018.
Digital Remains - poems of 2013 Beatlick Press 2018.
Broken Garden & The Unsaid Sings - poems of 2011 and 2012
    Beatlick Press 2015.
Hot Art & Other Plays - (collected plays) duende press 2019.
A New Land & Other Writings - (collected prose) duende press 2019.

=¦=

Here On Earth - 59 Sonnets La Alameda Press 1996.
Out of Secrecy - poems by Larry Goodell Yoo-Hoo Press 1992.
Firecracker Soup - poems 1980-1987 Cinco Puntos Press 1990.
Seven Sonnets - duende press 1987.
The Mad New Mexican - (Songs 1981-86) Ubik Sound 1986.
Dawn Ladder - San Marcos Press 1981?
Sunlove Gypsy - (mimeo) duende press 1967.
Cycles - author's first book, edited and with a foreword by
    William (Latif) Harris, (mimeo) duende press 1966.

Website, blogs http://www.larrygoodell.com/
Spoken word archives & music https://duende.bandcamp.com/
Videos http://bitly.ws/aoWU   https://twitter.com/larrygoodell

DUENDE PRESS
    the original - established 1964
cover photography and design by Lenore Goodell

BREATH

Breath. iv
Preface v
Note from Gary Brower v
The Light No Stars 2000 1
Ken 1
Stand By the Source. 2
A Piece 2
Smaller Worlds 3
In the Middle of the Night 3
Parked in the Garage. 4
Budding. 6
Just A Piece of Peace 6
Troubled 6
Play the Game 7
Two Parts of the Same Thing 7
Sloth 7
Open Ancestors 8
Praise. 8
Helping Our House Be Nice 9
The Magic Knob. 9
Enjoy Life 10
Out of Itself 11
Visitation 11
Up From Sleep 12
Song. 12
Move Over 12
Sublime Teacher 13
Breathe Easier 13
Intensity Too 14
Listening, for Delon. 15
The Earth and The Heavens 16
A Flow 17
Lighter Times Will Flow 17
Easter Sunday 2000 18
Duo-Mono 19
After Sunset 20
Path. 21
Towards Sunset 11th of July 21
Dance of the Atmosphere 22
In Your Service. 22
Stars, Lead Me 23
Move Over 23
Dancing in Now We Trust 24
Just The Best. 25
My Mind Is A Garbage Truck 25
Bury the Lie 26
Duties 27
Cloud of Knowing 28
History of the West 29
Servants of the Earth 30
Busy Going Noplace. 30
The Last Party on Earth. 31
Minimum Wages 31
Let Out 32
Outside-Inside 33
Flow. 34
Oh Cabezon 2001 35
Winter 35
Prayeritis. 35
from Heartbeat. 35
Coolest 36
Sloth Kill 36
Open To 37
Earth Love. 37
Moon Jump. 37
The Well of Turquoise. 38
Flower. 40
Sam Schwartz. 40
Mind 41
True Self 41
Waiting At BCDC. 41
Spring 42
Wet Body 42
In Secrecy 42
Beast in Man. 42
Bowl. 43
A Lesson in Listening 43
Tiny Tinies 44
The Truth of it All 44
Sunlight Light. 45
All I Have 46
No Mystery 46

Freely 47	Powerless and Free 83
Plantation of Real 48	Emptiness is Not Enough 84
Mood Elevators of the Dharma . . 48	El Malpais. 84
Tell Me 49	Sober Bartender. 85
Wild Hungarians. 50	Practice. 85
The Happy Poultry Club. 50	Last Play 86
A Piece of Your Peace of Mind. . . 51	Riddle 86
Entranced. 52	Breath, Feather, Fresh Air 87
The Joy of Rejecting 53	*from* The Direction of One. 88
Head Over Heels 54	In My Jungle Home 89
After Suns. 55	Is It True? 89
Flower Again 55	Start Off 90
Face In My Food 56	Cliche Exploded. 92
Crushing Ego Wars 57	At Last 92
Between Us Sings 58	Morning After Thanksgiving 92
Touched 60	Dance Slowly 93
Listening Love 61	Lonely. 93
Precious Wisdom 61	Result of Meditation 93
Breeze Speaks 62	I Shot Clarity 94
Over Pop Stranglehold 63	**Breath 2002**. 95
What Ever Happened to Fine. . . . 63	Red Dust. 95
Summer 64	Such As It Is 96
Happiness is a Thrill 64	Loneliness Lit Up 97
I Am Nature 64	Confession Confusion. 98
Drug 67	Unconscious Sonnet 99
Discourse While Eating 67	Steps 100
Love Appears 67	Guide 100
Are You a Bodhisattva?. 68	In Medias Res. 101
Exotic Enchantress 69	Closer 101
Morning Tea 70	Eulalia Hope 102
Heavenly Blue 71	Sad Story 104
New Breath 72	Fish Story 105
Down the Drain, A Holy Book. . . 74	The Greatest Story on Earth. . . . 106
Fall 75	Quote 106
Oh When I Die 75	In One Place. 107
The Art of Life 79	Brilliant End. 108
Goodbye. 75	Shock Talk 108
True Love 76	Pre-Dawn Dance 109
Mormon 76	Charm. 109
Solar Heat. 77	Talk 109
Anthrax Avenue. 78	Bad Day 110
And We Thought Gertrude Stein 79	Good Day 110
A Bit of Peace. 80	Hairnet 111
Living in the Problem 81	Thinking Straight 111
Unchained Melody 82	In the Calm 112

Just Is	114	Epithalamium	140
Creation Plus	114	July Twenty Second	141
Something Was Inspiring	115	Feminine Ending	142
American Portrait	116	Tough Turkey	143
No Strings Attached	116	Root Level	144
Her Cue	116	A Pastoral	145
We're Innocent	117	The Round Robin of Love	145
To the Old Pope	117	For the Cowboy Buddha	146
Interrelation	117	Making Up Places	147
Literal	117	Wishful Stinking	148
What the Heck	118	War and Peace	148
First	118	Die Oh Log	148
For My Closest	119	Some Call It Grace	149
Companion	119	Ass First Through the Cosmos	149
Death Spurt	120	Just For Fun	149
Right On	121	Under Stars	150
Jazz Set Me Free	121	Coloratura Bossa Nova	151
First Breath	122	A Big Meeting	152
Mutual	122	My Ego	154
One On One	123	Gift Giving	155
Pray, That Is To Say	123	Stampede of Morons	155
Sold For Profit	124	Eating the Light	156
A Japanese Sensibility	125	Meditations	156
Robber	126	Coming Out of It	157
Drama of the Heart	126	Hummingbirds	158
A Perspective	127	Cartoon	158
Bats	127	Partners Return	159
Glad	128	Moon Haiku	159
Seeing Drink	128	Whole	160
Hands	129	Enlightenment Is the Patootie	160
Connected	129	Now A Muse	161
Right Now Alien	130	A Body Discovered	161
G.O.D.	130	Image Nation	162
Fighting Big Egos To the End	131	A Gentleman Beggar	163
Just Friends	132	Hum Joy	163
On the Way	132	Fall Morning Glory	164
The Wood	133	Reality Note	164
Relax Into Me	134	Lubriderm	165
Good	134	Screw Loose Logic	165
Limbo Dust	134	What Is It	166
Greater Than Reality	135	Roswell North	166
With One Heart (To Song)	136	Eons Speak	167
Turning My Back	137	Love Evolve	167
My Piece of Flying Saucer	138	In The Stars	168
Simplicity	139	I Don't Know Spanish	172

Moist Italians	173	Poetry Lite	190
In the Media Conquistadors	174	Hole	191
Take Me Up	175	Compost	192
Creator	175	Doors	193
Found In Roswell	176	Tinkerer	193
Orion More	176	An Even Dozen	194
Heavenly Blessed	177	Back Down	194
Dance	177	The Troot	195
Walter Beckwith	177	On The Tip of the Tongue	195
Baby Brain	178	Orgopoopia	195
Top of the List	179	Alien Classified	196
Democratic Joy	180	Minimum Wages	198
Surprise	182	Permission to be True	198
Wide Open	184	Diagram of Love	199
Gondalay	185	Notes	200
Renewable Energy	185	Index	201
Voice Present	186	Comments	204
The Eternal Muse Not Arrogant	188	Recent Books	205
The Eternal Muse Does Not Kill	188		

BREATH

My heartbeat
    the creator.
My breath,
    gratitude.

PREFACE

Bringing my work to press is a project I call *Hear*. Starting in 2015 and ongoing I published in 7 books my work from 2000 to 2019, including my plays - *Hot Art* - and my prose - *A New Land*. The first were from Beatlick Press and subsequent books from Duende. *Breath*, the newest, brings together poems from 2000, 2001 and 2002. I'm 85 and plan to continue with my rather problematic-to-publish performance work of the early 70's. Other books such as Jim Fish's poems are craving publication. Time and life gift will tell.

I started Duende Press with a mimeo machine in '63 here in Placitas but then I learned offset and continued to publish small books and magazines of poet and artist friends off and on. Friends have published my *Cycles, Dawn Ladder, The Mad New Mexican (songs), Out of Secrecy, Firecracker Soup,* and *Here On Earth* as well as poems in many friendly magazines. All along there were poetry events to organize and promote in Albuquerque, Bernalillo and Placitas. Lenore, photographer and artist, has added a vision of strength to my life and an active appreciation of pre-Columbian art and sculpture, flowering native flora, and the beauty of Planet Earth when left unviolated.

I am hopeful these are writings that reach beyond myself to be read and, when read, are sometimes read aloud. The poems are mostly freely given "dramatic monologues" or simply one person scores. -LG

NOTE FROM GARY BROWER

"Nature is . . . a common theme in Goodell's poetry: the role of Nature, the need to save the planet from destruction by corporate greed, the beauty of walking in the Ojito Wilderness, the yearly gardens around his house, his tasks with the local acequia committee to clean out irrigation canals, the stark beauty of the Sandia foothills, the timeless poetry of the "fervent valley" where he lives, above the larger Rio Grande Valley, in the shadow of the Cosmic Mountain. We think you will find all these riches in the poetry of Larry Goodell." -GB

From the *Malpais Review,* Summer 2012,"Mythic & Secular Rituals of an Anglo *Koshare* Poet in Placitas," in which Goodell was a featured poet.

THE LIGHT
NO STARS ARE MADE OF

2000

KEN
/for Ken Irby (1936-2015)

I have missed the delight of your height of intellect
missed stretching my mind to your pathways,
missed the leap of discovery only an American can make
as it comes from you and the eternal muse,
missed the intense layers of surfaced history
as your stories of this continent interconnect
    with you, with me . . . .
The rightness in the faith in our tongue
from the heartland, from the corn and wheat land,
from the planet's crosscurrents of mystery and myth
    of your Chinese and Europe
        and all the arts
in your genius of knowhow
    and the risk of words and song
        discovering you
the wine and pleasure of instant gratitude
we shared together – friendship above all, calls. /5Jan

STAND BY THE SOURCE

Will I ever find the Stars at my elbow?
The Moon in my throat?
The Sun I walk on?
The Earth in my heart?
Will I ever be as simple as that?
Following my thoughts to reality?
The dog follows me in and then the cat
here by the fire in the living room.
They are both lying on the rug.
I am standing by the fire.
We just like being together.
The dog and the cat and the man in the moon,
will it ever be as simple as that?

A PIECE

Faith is the bridge to serenity
as if I had any faith, any serenity –
I certainly have the bridge, I'm
a moving bridge to something all the time.
By giving my decision-making up
I'm letting someone else run the show –
    Fate, God, Higher Source, Random Chance?
So I do have faith in lack of direction,
full-blown faith.
I'll let things move along their course today –
letting go gives me some ease.
So I do have faith in my lack of direction.
Infuse me with instant knowhow, when I need it
and lead to a piece of peace of mind.

SMALLER WORLDS

Is good and evil one?
I don't have a degree in what I'm thinking.
Moral philosophy, moral anything.
　　The philosophy of the Spirit. The path. The way.
The divided path isn't divided, but is intertwined.
　　Why do I think anything. Try to
address my better self. I can't improve
if I'm not going from A to B.
I have to improve from this point of confusion –
　　growth, to *something*. I'm too dumb
to know any different.
Something informs me, Move on.
　　*Go without a goal, except
　　　enjoyment of change.* Snaking along
addressing my better self, from change to change
surprise alright. So why is everything
　　so much the same?
　　Smaller worlds every day.
Perhaps this is the way.

IN THE MIDDLE OF THE NIGHT

What's wrong with me is disturbing.
The key to the sunshine in my heart.
What the poet tells. My dark side is my light side.
Or they're so close one stumbles on the other.
I see what isn't imposed on what is.
Everything that should be, in my mind, isn't,
as more rain comes than snow on Earth here
and we're being warmed to death.
The better self says "Wait, it is your father's will."
And I say, I hear my mother complain.
Father Sky doesn't necessarily know what's best for Mother Earth.
They're working together in ways I don't know.
Maybe too many humans will work itself out.
Here in the middle of the night. I await the sunlight.

PARKED IN THE GARAGE OF THE FUTURE

I said it was a Real Thing.

If I'm happy it's because the shower of "the grace of God"
washed down on me as I was driving up
    the narrow road under that hanging-over
        cottonwood tree
            on the way back
        from a meeting in which
    all things came together,
    the *tone* was right
    the *time* open
    the relaxation anointed into tranquillity
    sarong dance Rita Hayworth
    serenity
nothing to do with the real world
God came together
God is simply
the Earth
an old Taos guy with a gravelly voice
told me over the radio
over the rainbow
under the tree
driving free
just you and me
my tranquility
my let go let go –
my gift of gab
turned into real words
I listen to
listening is free
to turn into this gift
you round world around me
me driving through
to collapse at home
into being known by you, *real world god leader*
    director saint mudhead universal star, shawl
    draped over the continent of my stars . . .

I simply accept the nature in my self
untrammeled by fights of argument orgasms
red faces and puke
free free free in the Sober state of Reality –
Father, Mother of Earth, I'm yours
you said "Go forth just be,
you're a pretty happy guy if you just
    rely on me."
Anything that's not this easy state of grace
    is fake, put-on, ass-holery, begone!
I'm here in the love that always is
the more I accept it the more
it turned to me
    I'm in it,
    deep mystery
    unknown known
    the fabric of destiny,
    Hollywood dance number
        combined in a Western
    with an unending plot
        Play on!
    Wild Rite of Passage
    through the sunset gates, the pillars of
        climbing roses
            growing up over
        the garage of the future
    I'm parked in now –
I feel good
now I've said it.
Stay there
in simple terms
be your true self.
    Aha!
Ha.

(This happened last evening driving home after the Placitas Sunday Night meeting, right on the road at Fritz's house.)

BUDDING

When you keep asking for it
it comes
keep opening the door
something walks in
even if it's your higher self.
This is the budding presence
the flower of the universe
among many billion
that is yours
or mine to open to
as *it* is opening. /1Feb

JUST A PIECE OF PEACE

More than that
it is more than that
and yet the self same thing
that I am
as part of
and that as part of
everything
is part of.   /1Feb

TROUBLED

Enter in
oh enter alien in
oh enter stranger in
oh enter friend in –
no door barred if
you are who you are.
You have a difficulty? Welcome
enter in./4Feb

PLAY THE GAME

What's the difference Chula Vista
What's the difference?
What's the difference acne paranoid
What's the difference?
What's the difference psychotic
    peace and serenity
What's the difference?
What's the difference up and down
    in and out why shout?
What's the difference?
If the universal one is a pun
what's the difference.
If more Gods than one
what's the difference?
If you and I the same
what's the difference?
Play the game.

TWO PARTS OF THE SAME THING

You are having a good day.
Don't let anybody take it away.
Especially that other half of your brain
which seems to exist only to complain.

SLOTH

Sloth is a very big monster
which sucks you into nothing.
I've been there many times before
doing
nothing
not even aware of nothing
but *doing*
nothing.

OPEN ANCESTORS

    Open Ancestors.
    Open Padre, the Madre.
   Be Father to the Mother
   Mother to the Mother –
loose chains of ancestors
call to the new ones
"It's your turn,
your turn to turn."
I hear unknown Grandfathers
to my Grandfathers
Grandmothers also saying
 "You did the best we did.
  We did the best we could.
   You can do the best you can.
   You do the best we did.
    You can do the best you do.
    We did the best you did."
     I hear Grandmothers of the Grandfathers
     sons and sons and sons of daughters
     daughters of Grandmothers
    saying down to me,
    "That is all you do
   What you do for me.
   You do what yourself knows
  and you do it free.
  When this you speak
 do it after me.
What you do is yours alone
and thus you are free."

PRAISE

Apricot blossoms on the manure heap.
What blessing of the digestive system!

HELPING OUR HOUSE BE NICE

Love in your focus on what you're up to
    and carrying it through.
We tore out, or rather you took out
the bathroom cabinets, drained and took out
the fish tank, put together linen closets
and cabinet for the bathroom sink
and we bought big sheets of dry wall and
    cement wall and toted them to truck
and then from truck to house.
And still you had energy because you
were following the Order of Love.

THE MAGIC KNOB

The pretentiousness of the ego is bigger than God
and even if you have no God
it's bigger than an elephant caravan.
A man's ego is bigger that a woman's, more destructive,
bigger than the worst calamity toward others.
And woman's ego can be so big
ships sail under it, in the wrong direction
and all the gods clash in the super stars of heaven,
the multi galaxies of the last gasp of the universe –
man-gods and woman-gods trying to drum up an ego
bigger than man's and woman's, the human species has
the biggest head, bigger than creation and destruction.

No god can compete with human ego –
self-fulfilling, self-enduring, self-made
self-righteous, self-fumigating, self-molding
self seeking self, self-sucking, self-feeding
self-preening self-coddling self-exploding
self all over the place, weaving in and out of self
    adoring self self-defending self-cheering
self-smearing self-insisting self-demanding, self
    taking over the world and then worlds of worlds
till there's no end except destruction, destruction
of self turned to shit as they get up from the toilet. /21Feb

ENJOY LIFE

     Entering the Godhead
What do you find?
     No Mormon shrine
or Protestant or Catholic engulfment
     but the sheerest possible entry into
     things as they are
     never changed by a guitar
     or drink in a bar
     or caviar
     but what is is
     the present is the future and the past
     the great now warms to your presence
     and informs
     like a wind blowing over
     the wind blowing across
     reminds me of itself
     and becomes everything
     I do know now
     what little bit of peace.
     I hear the pump pumping warm water
         through the floors
         warming the bricks
         I feel with my feet
as the white globe above my head
illuminates the message –
I'm safest when in the end
I don't pretend
 and find humorous
  just about everything
   that doesn't anger –
    little corny jokes
     along the way.
      Big heads
       have no place
       in reality
        as I try to see
        without one.

Just an ordinary head
not even a God head.
Please!
Let's not joke about enjoying life.
I'm grounded in the Earth
with my head in the clouds
and my belly rumbling.

OUT OF ITSELF

The Universe is the Creator
    Created.
What came before the Created
    is a Spiritual Unknown
the Heights of Machu Picchu
    ascended.
More sacred than Everest
    is the dawn
we can all realize
and everything creates itself
    with the day
and relaxes, repose
    at night.
It is simple
    when I say it is so –
sometimes I believe
    myself.
Is *that* so?

It is simple as that bird
gliding across my sight
from left to right.
The day creates itself
so that it may be so
it is so or seems so
to be so.
A car driving by,
the music in the other room,
the breeze outside,
the dog barking, this intense
morning gray-blue light
on which I can write
anything,
in which I can live
a life.
Spring forth
like creation.

VISITATION

Creator is a reckless wanderer
who enters my vagabond soul
and settles me down
as he ambles on.

UP FROM SLEEP

Every thought is prayer
every prayer is thoughtless
unless it is to the true self
which is from higher mind
which is connected
to supreme action
in "transfigured night"
"a little night music"
which is the other hand of day
of dawn and delight in
accomplishment of the great
which started from the small –
two hands clapping
or none at all.
The beginning of everything
by knowing nothing
and yet not dumb –
strength takes exercise
and active thoughts.
Activating thoughts
refreshes the body,
activating body
refreshes thoughts.
Slowing down
speeds up night.
Prayer is thoughtless
unless posited on
creative speaking
from the true self
up from the new which is
old as night:
what may I do for you?

SONG

Real life sings
without a deception –
the breathing in and out
without the light
is death and deception.

MOVE OVER

As the sun comes up the Earth turns
to kiss me.
Am I so special? No
I just happen to be in the way.

SUBLIME TEACHER

Nature is the sublime teacher
reaching every turnabout of my solo body
as the plum blossoms in full bloom
    attract the bees
I pick up clothes on the ground
from the blown-down clothes line. /19Mar

BREATHE EASIER

Out of desperation comes
the voiceless voice of my heart
asking for help when
any decision I make seems
hopeless or wrong *or* confused.
I can't make *any* decision.
I give up and that's that.
All the bad that someone endures
does not have to make me
all bad.
The goodness is my separation
from it.
So that I can be stronger
if not strong,
saner
if not sane.
At peace
if not serene.
Functional
if not organized.
In tune with others
if not pleasantly sociable.
Get back to my own focus –
"You're in the fix
you got yourself into."
And what can I do –
stand out of the way
and breathe easier.

INTENSITY TOO

Time may go by singing apples freely
and the Earth unmend from too many people,
but still in Spring our Almond with
    its full bloom perfume
will carry me to the edge of Earth and beyond.
Memories of what is sweetest become real
as I pass on in the spirit where I can live with them.
The sensation of Earth alive breathing freely
gives rise to hope which gives rise to faith
which gives rise to the inevitability of Spirit,
the clarity of good air and water dashed on
    my forehead in the morning
and then to my reading "to watch loneliness vanish"
    and then to prayer to take me as I go
through the paradoxes of the day as pure as
    yesterday's falling aslant snow –
such myriads of fluffs dizzying, down
in springtime no less
and the clouds turning the mountain
    into a dramatic uplift backlit backdrop
        earlier in the day.
It all sings to say "Protect me, allow me growth
not just you humans today."
And I said in the snow, Thank you, thank you
for allowing me to live on your planet for awhile.
May I clean up after myself,
may I foster like a gardener, your presence.

I better *be* the gardener I am
and get my hands dirty to help you grow.
Real tomatoes we have started and now starting peppers
    bell and jalapeño
and searching through the seeds for broccoli
    and other seeds from previous years' store.

What is real and imagined mixes in this instant.
May I make some little things better
    by not doing too much
to change beauty which is already there.

Earth breathes in relief when I
    don't outstep boundaries
which I do all the time I am not real
but follow a foolish fantasy.
I am important as Nature Mother Dawn
    Father Creator
when actually the intense almond in full bloom
    covered with last evening's snow
excites my memories there is hope
there may be fruit yet
(apples haven't even bloomed).
So much is in bud besides the almond perfume
besides what's in my head –
    much more to everything. /1Apr

LISTENING
    /for Delon

As soon as I woke up I heard the revelation of the stars.
"Be a Buddha, be Christian, be oriented to the East,
eat cheese. Go out late at night but come back.
Eat cake and good food. Be regular.
Don't tend to anything frolicsome unless it's children
    or kittens or puppies.
Don't do anything right until you learn to do something right
    by doing it all the time.
Don't listen to me until your ears are open, your speech wet
    your saliva tangy, your heart pure.
Be who you are right now, now you are right now.
Now you are what you are right now, that is becoming
    alive, always at the same time presently alive.
    On the path along the way in process of discovery
be discovery. Don't be anything. Don't listen to the stars.
You don't have to. You're asleep when they're talking to you."
As soon as I woke up I heard the revelation of the stars.
Enjoy life take risks but don't hurt anybody.
Energy energy energy: "Go out and pretend that you
    got good sense."

THE EARTH AND THE HEAVENS
THE MOON AND THE STARS

Everything is in rainbow mode.
There's no mist but there's reliable sun.
Imagination parades before me in reality.
What is more beautiful than Spring
    when there's no wind
    as this morning dances around.
The cherries just coming out
the apples swelling to bloom
the plums clustered with white blossoms
    and the bees out early.
Oh the luxury of out of work living
retired or pretending to be so!
I'm having such a swell time sitting,
a little reading writing looking at
narcissus and tulips and grape hyacinth
    parading around.
It's nice when there aren't so many insects
except the buzzing bees.
The parade of my heart
the parade of the moon unseen.
My luxury of time.
I don't deserve to have all this
and yet the dance goes on.
The vaulting parade of the morning
    progresses as I look down
at the fruit tree floats
and the colors of the Earth
vibrate up with the dancers
bend into rainbows over
Delius, Mozart, Astor Piazzolla
and the wild plums' white surprise.

Clouds now veil the sun
and a chill sets in.
Where has it gone: everything waits
in paradise.

A FLOW

Love is outgoing
ongoing though I don't catch myself
    flowing with it.
Lately, the last day, I have,
and now listening over headphones
    to Mozart wind quintet
I feel love outflowing
    from his true sense.

LIGHTER TIMES WILL FLOW

In times of light and times
lighter times will flow
where heavier the spirits
heavier times dominate
but that will come and go.

In the waiting room waiting for Lenore to finish her visit

EASTER SUNDAY 2000

It's all gone dead dying out
the fresh memories that live only in my mind.
I relive them in flashes
but the distance kills me
so when I hum Stardust
it's my mother, teaching me to play the piano
playing that piece as I learned it.
And when I think of San Antonio Rose
I think of my dad now weak, now old.
My mother is long dead
but my home family life, that home of Roswell
that family – the concatenation of images sing
through my mind
faces and places and clothes,
private to me and to die with me
when that is.

Thanks for having me over for dinner
over and over, family
of youth and friends and family
of friends.
You are all gone now, except the fringe
of what's left.
Dad, I hope you survive this latest onset of age.
May we renew ourselves by talking about
the shared things in times passed.
Time has passed
leaving those picnics in the backyard by
the wishing well and clothesline
and flowering yucca and gardens of my mother
and all that ham and chicken and hamburgers and hotdogs
and those iceberg lettuce salads with pale tomatoes
and all those pies, apple, peach, lemon, chocolate and
    the memory fades.

Now my family is so oddball and strange
and near and dear
that it's hard to talk about it to my dad.

Are they married? he asks
   You have a granddaughter?
I have to remind him, families are thoroughly
different and were
long before this new century.

We didn't have a picnic
but we ate out at the Range
blue corn chicken enchiladas red chile, green chile
chef's salad, ice tea, bubblegum soda
and little Lyra loved her salad, good green lettuce
and good red tomato
and took her chicken fingers home
and this is as good as we ever can do.

My son and I went to Easter Sunday church together –
it just happened, against my will.
But when I was a kid, it was
common practice.
I remember I was baptized on Easter Sunday.
Now, anything of the old memories
that allows me to live them again
is a reminder, it doesn't all die.
I think, I thank, give out love as best I can.
To live in the resurrection
of the moment.

DUO-MONO

"Wherever I go I see God"
   What does God look like?
"God looks like Reality."
   What is the difference between
   God and Reality?
"God infuses Reality with Spirit
   and leaves it more or less
   the way it was."

AFTER SUNSET

I experience God in his not being present.
And in his place there is a power,
    a magnificence and grace.
    As the sky fills up with itself
    and the sun goes down
grays take over, distant blues, glows.
The hill to my right slopes up out of sight
the apple and pear trees to my left and tall spruce.
The Austrian copper rose in bloom, dim,
    directly ahead of me as I sit on this portal
framing all, darkening into bird calls
and the dog listening.
Crickets.
The power takes over, the magnificence
    of changing day
and the grace of acceptance.
I blend with reality and do not interpose.
The real leads me by the nose.
I sit in it.
The white vinyl chair.
The distant Jemez.
The old volcanic flow.
Time that goes, that goes.
Nothing is happening
while everything is being itself
in living and dying.
Energy poised to my hearing
 take from me my difficulties
  that I may see you better.
   Things as they are
    guide me.
     As it is *now*
      the magnificence of living by degree
      in the grace of growth,
       the defeat of the lazy lout in me
       setting me, my truer self, free.
        As dark light comes and fades away.

PATH

    Some days I go from one glorious instance
      to another
   other days I'm scraping the bottom of the barrel.
    Am I bi-polar in flights and depths?
 No, I'm tri-polar.
 I'm now in the middle, just being here
being here, aware of the ups and downs
the tenuousness of these great glorious bounds
  where the world breathes freely
  and I follow.
    Perhaps I'm there now, and don't know it.
    which is everywhere.
    Let it be.
    Let it be free to be . . .

    Clean up the kitchen.
    Cut down that alfalfa.
    Get a turkey coop set up.
    Take that trash to the dump
   and apologize to Mother Earth.
   And thank your lucky stars
  for being all the stars
  which you can only see
a small, small number
in rich astounding diversity
in the night of your imagining.

TOWARDS SUNSET 11TH OF JULY

I found a sky bigger than I can see. I found the wind seeming to caress. I made honest statements to everything I looked at. You are what you are and if I'm being honest I don't experience anything like "God" – only "what is." Last night I kept looking at the sky and no matter where I looked I could only see a part, looked up and out at every direction and could never see the whole thing. My periphery won't allow. Then I realized that a higher power is always there part of and beyond what I see.

DANCE OF THE ATMOSPHERE

I lived my life on the cuff
sailing through the precipice of air
till age crept up in the vacuum of my skull
waiving everything
and the star of discovery appeared
     and conjured up Earth
          out of the materials of the leftover universe
and we got together in a body
and the mind came back and formed a brain
and all myths arose in the early morning, dawn
     of sex and suddenly
     love.
So on this glad Earth, there's a chance
a brief chance to do it right
a brief chance to help someone else
imagine the dance of the atmosphere
and then breathe in reality
     a brief chance
     a brief chance
a breath of the miracle of air.

IN YOUR SERVICE

Does the heterodox boogie-woogie wagon say hello?
Earth times of Earth Spirits say so.
Open the mouths of the open mouths' volcanic roar.
Muses, Spirits, Dice Lines, movements to and fro
Through the Vacuum of Paradise: Trust and
Your Trust will be refurbished. The hidden
Doctrine of the Sphinx under the left paw
Under the Temple to the Moon outside Mexico City.
The Temple to the world's greatest buffoon.
Expositorio. Impressario. The Human Ego.
Let's dance and let it all out in a new way.
Dance off superiority. I am at Your Service.
She dances by in Your Service. I follow turning waving
Bending. In Your Service. I bow without scraping.

STARS, LEAD ME

Stars, lead me to the light no stars are made of
and I can live there in the place of poverty,
poverty meaning my spirit stripped of ego,
living in your sound, your sensation of intellect
your architecture of going.

You surround me with a way to go
when I hesitate.
When love seems all, all I can do
comes rushing like a Clear Creek from Colorado.
Take me, move me, direct me
in Nature's full delight.
Take me with you through folding doors
    of the outside world
the cathedral of the breath and heart worth knowing.
Love rushes on, and let it go,
in a church urgent with
ordinary light.

MOVE OVER

"The human world is a global penis to screw Nature
    and fuck God.
It took a helluva lot of aggressive work
    to turn Mother Nature into a big cunt,
a helluva lot of men and a lot of women
to masculinize everything –
the Moon turned into a prop for further planetary buggery,
Mars into a platform for us to dominate.
Our human ego and pride rides the horse of violent destiny –
greed dominates our spirit, what more species do we need
    but ours, really?
That's why we overpopulate, to kill off everything.
Nature is in the way of God the Man.
Move over, rest of the world, rest of the universe, rest of
    whatever's left
move over and be poked."

DANCING IN NOW WE TRUST

for Maryann Threadgill

I gotta be free
and be healing
feeling the just
and the fair
    I gotta be willing
    wondering
    appealing
    to the goodness
    we all share
I gotta be open
to the best
go with the winners
and then trust
    I gotta be knowing
    I can be flowing
    with and not against
    the just and fair
I have loving
I have going
I have singing
and revealing
    I have eating
    and repeating
    looking sinking
    fair and square
I gotta be open
to new knowing
gotta be honest
in all things
gotta be trusting
as in trusted
gotta try
to be aware
here in love
there in friendship
in we go
to more than we know
    the time is ripe
    simply not gripe
    to see it now
    as never before
to just be faithful
do what I say
when I say
I will do
    you can trust
    I'll be there too
    you and me we'll
    see it through
best is best
I follow after.
Let's be true to
one another
    and be all we
    can in life
    and it's a good
    ole direction
dancing where
we were once
dancing in
now we trust.   /7Sep

JUST THE BEST
for Maryann

Is it gossip, is it knowing, is it telling the facts?
Is it keeping the stories alive?
Is it just a little history, just a little life
just a little humor, wild and nice?
Just a little memory, just a little spice
just a little humping by the white buffalo?
Just a little story of what goes on
behind the fancy shades of a summer life?
Tell it all as only you can
 keep us knitted together.

That's the best
here out West
how the best was won oh yes!
How the best was won.
Won and told
Won and told
How the best was won!

MY MIND IS A GARBAGE TRUCK

Consciously a big ole dump truck
    full of head garbage –
I pull the lever and the bed of the truck lifts
        and empties out.
I pull the lever and my mind empties out.
What flows in is the beginning of the day,
    this way, dawn comes clean.
All this is above me, beyond me,
I only *ask* and I'm emptied out today.

BURY THE LIE

There's no front to the front
but the back shows through.
The side touches the side
and the up and down are one.
Are you superior if four is more important than one?
Or one is more important than three?
Or does two make you see through things?
Or is the five-pointed star your last recall?
What color is your huevos rancheros?
Are you blind to being deaf to music?
Or can't you hear what you see? See?
All things being equal, reality.
No ideas but in smorgasbords unless you're Swedish
and then you'll know something about your past.
Or are you an indigenous wafer
tossed here by an outerspace company?
At root everything is commercial.
God carries advertisement signs for the latest trend
which is Buddha.
Buddha sees eye to eye with the Pope who has
holdings in Nova Scotia.
The world is a great big Buy Buy Buy.
Buy anything but buy if you're a man,
preferably guns.
Don't shoot the rich but aim to stamp out poverty.
I'm the voice of the voice behind the voice.
I'm clutter and ego, the past and the future.
Instead drop all of this and look in the mirror
that does not reflect back.
What speaks has no face and turns into everything.
The play of wisdom, the play of the play
the game of truth, the cottontail scampering from the garden
the full moon with waves of clouds racing over it
and three stars that might be planets seeming to race by.
Everything is movement plus, energy and change
and saying nothing beats everything I've heard.
But one thing only and that's not theater or the stage
but the play within the play with the bad and the good
and the up and the down.

Listen to me quick and get up and sit,
stand and run
do nothing and all, things will come to you
as they've never come to you.
Bend to the source, the birth of stars
time ordinary. Resist thinking.
Dawn will bring light to someone else.
Take an axe to your ego. That's right
split wood to start winter fires.
Do you see the dawn yet carrying on?
It's early in the middle of the night.
Somewhere a black beetle is trying to get out of the house
but he doesn't know it.
She knows everything and she
put down his gun to have a good time.
It's okay if you plan it big
respecting the planet.
Everything is blank, at night
the same as our source.
Popped out didn't it, at you, the light?
Don't laugh, but it's so funny.
If it's tragic take it seriously
if you can help somebody.
Don't listen to me, I'm past hope
and then afterward what a story!
Live lightly but be of use. Be free.
"The Play of Mystery" it says on my tombstone.

DUTIES

I got up and there was a potato that hadn't been baked
I got up and there was a bean that hadn't been boiled
I got up and there was a pea that hadn't been eaten
I got up and there was a word that hadn't been written.

CLOUD OF KNOWING

He stepped on the cloud of knowing
and unleashed from within was the flowing
from all directions out and in, up and around
down down down and from within the secret
unlocked never locked, was nature
the nature of it all as all outdoors was in
was within his inward self not in the brain
in the body-brain, the soul train, the bus belly
the jet groin, the auto heart the voice of love
the love of silence where the wind comes up
and *touches* and the warmth of blood flowing
beating like the drum from the party down the road
indistinguishable, inextinguishable, became him
came from within to become him, transcend *him*
guide, flow, serene power to float on, to be
is, was, it was his nature all along, sexless, paternal
maternal, eternal, male in female, a lift
a bargain, a knowing step in the right direction
as clean as sober as warm as clasped hands
as assuring, reassuring as friendly talk in the night
as friendly work in the day, as to pray from within
to let it out, inspiration in his hearing when all
was lost, the listening in the ears opening to it
hearing what he saw in the sunset in the middle of the night –
wind whispering come back to yourself, it is not selfish
to own a corner of the universe for a lifetime, to look within
to open to guide to accept command to live and grow
to give, down on your knees, thanks for the spirit
breath breathing soul-spirit, true spirited self
the relaxing entry, the door open, the love contained the love
freed, at long last freed within to be redeeming in itself
planned unplanned hoped accepted admitted life
of the force of discovery originality from the origin of things
no things but in ideas, no ideas but the force of nature
from within, the quiet that hears, hears itself, hears
what it says, it says nothing and allows you
to say honestly purely as real spring water
willingly and openly love yourself as you are

as you are love, you are yourself, your body-idea
 living as each thing is full of energy of the combination
of universes in each instance now simply within
to love all things from this vibrant center nature out.

=⁚=

HISTORY OF THE WEST

To have a burning cowpuncher experience
where the tumbleweed bursts into flame
the aurora of darkness turns into
    rainbows of your dreams
the gloomiest night vision turns over into a sunset
where archetypal dramas are played out in an instant
where white light speaks from the horse's eyes,
where the turning of everything turns into the
    turning of everything over the fire
fried, boiled, roasted by the Cook.
Burning white light golden yellow bright
    sudden transformation of the West into
    the East and all directions –
an entire change from one reality to another.
Me naked sitting under three 75 watt bulbs
reflected in the bathroom mirror 2 o'clock at night.
As bright as bright is
drained of the imagination.
Free of storytelling.
As naked as the sister of God
as true as the son of the local high school football coach
    and as relevant.
A family of vision centered in reality
marching off into the sunset.
Everything imagined at once and dropped –
    never to be forgotten
for at least one lifetime, for at least one night
for a connection with past time future –
the sensation of whitest light
in the womb of blackest night.

SERVANTS OF THE EARTH

    Human intellect had lost it's heart
     and was living on in a furious shell of itself
     thinking thinking thinking it knew everything
    when in reality it was
    thinking itself to death.

    Bat God, or the prior Intellect of the Universe
   that was all of the potential heart of love
   intertwined in a non-dualistic caring reality
  reached down in intuition, imagination, art and prayer
 and picked up man's dead heart and mended it,
woman's dead heart and mended it, transformed it
so that it transcended the intellect and directed vision,
spoke at one with the Earth, the higher being's child,
at last again we think with our ears and can get back
     to our servant status
mending the Earth our intellects have
    all but destroyed.
How can we lessen ourselves?
   By listening.
"Let wealth crumble. The Earth will give you no more."
 Lessen ourselves and be servants to the Earth.
  Listening to the miraculous gift of Paradise
   as we are steered through the universe
    millennium by millennium.
     Lessen ourselves and be Servants of the Earth.

BUSY GOING NOPLACE

   You're not changing anything   you're staying the same
   you're stuck oiling your wheels   wheels going around
   not coming in contact   with the ground.

THE LAST PARTY ON EARTH
(harsh voice)

"Find your Dharma.
Stand up with the Sphinx.
Electro-vac your future.
Christian marbles and Buddhist fly swatters
 will change your life.
No longer need anything
Arguments are past.
Permanent smile tattoos available at the door.
The chandelier of cockroaches will be our pleasure.
Man, empty man dead in the coffin, will be our God.
Aren't you happier than you were
 when you cared about others?
  Isn't it a relief to shove the last bit of Nature left
  under our carpet of gold
and step on it as you lighten your pleasure.

Your ego tied to your millions is all we want.
Our egos are one and we call it fun.
We eat the desiccated memory of good
and fall down before the flag of urine.
Stench is our perfume, it's so nice to see you
we have everything of yours in our bank of misery. "

MINIMUM WAGES

What do ants make an hour?
What is the daily wage of a rhinoceros?
How much do birds get?
Those bees, do they get paid a lot?

LET OUT

Bless confess arrest the Dharma in you
in me bloated ego arrest nothing let go
you are the me of the hour
the instant of this second
I you me in my head, dead.
I call you I call me call me I,
digest my head.
Living I give life life by denying strife.
Everything hurts, I bloat.
I get on my knees and float.
Give up everything and you get nothing.
Something stronger than mere me protests
changes the vacuum of things.
God *loves* a vacuum because he enters in
and is immediately dissipated into the Buddha.
Buddha is bigger than God and won the fight –
    so that's settled.
Jesus is misinterpreted, Buddha has a big head.
Ego deflation arrests the Gods –
it finally got their attention.
Mother Superior rapped their knuckles with a ruler
and now that the Pope got a sex change
she is a mystery to all.
There is no mystery if you open your eyes
    your ears your touch your mind your heart –
and pray with the flow.
Stop lecturing, stop everything, stop trying to stop.
Freedom teaches me values.
Excess got me to enlightenment. ....
What is enlightenment? A word in the dictionary.
There's also another word in the dictionary
    and that's bail bond, whoops! two words.
There's always a surprise, no denying.
So don't bail the guy out, let him sit there
and experience the whys and wherefores.

So I sit here free again after having been in
    the jail of negativity most of my life
expressing positives to everyone while
    I was personally discombobulated.

Now I know the flow, the breathing lets go.
In deep and out, out there, is so
and gentle wind rustles the dried cottonwood leaves
in the big trees by the spring as water
    pushes up through the sand at the
bottom of the pool, my mind, and the wind
    I breathe through and get up refreshed
having had everything lifted over, freed
    to greater powers, design, structure than I'll
ever know. I know it. As the impossible speaks
through the leaves, the water, the endless flow
    goes away from me, and I can simplify
and find I don't find anything at all
    but trust. The only bank I bank on. Built up
foundation, mud layers, sky. I'm free to go.
Release can be slow but in this instant, now, I'm free to go.

 1

OUTSIDE-INSIDE

Evil is the exterior of God
the outside, shedding of the skin
the dead some reflection of light falls on
with human stirrings bringing it to life again.

And entering the interior, can grow in strength
till flung outward another time in space
by human effort of the good.
The persistence of energy for better
wins out in the full bodied joy of life
stepping beautiful naked forward
from the dead left behind.
Nature in all her glorious attributes
and the atmosphere of dawn kisses love into action.
Universal being as simple as her presence.   /25Dec

FLOW

Water, what is water.
 As pure as the earth when uncontaminated.
  The miracle, that is appreciation of the real
   water, the pure thing in all its disclosures.
    Clarity flows through water.
      I can't fathom it, I use it, try not to overuse.
      The miracle that is, the reality of one thing
      which makes life possible:
      everything is in consort.
     I pick up the baton if I am a conductor.
     Or if I'm Igor Stravinsky
    I hop on the podium and raise my hands and here we go.
   The first symphonic effect:
  light flows through water as the Mysterions play on.
A glistening effect.
Clarity of the God's mouth speaks.
There is a singing of all orifices.
The face faces off, relaxes,
      the head of the body of the hour lies back,
      all its openings open breathing
as the sun produces moisture in the atmosphere
and oxygenated air flows out and through
the creek, the stream, the water, the high lake, the delta
the river, rivulet, concordance of flows
 oceans of memory seas of landlocked mysteries.
  Time passes on as great canyons touch
   creation at their feet. The water I drink now
    I drink in now. Drinks astonishes fills completes
     and ever flows flows.
    The tea I spilled on the oak breakfast table
    spilled when I filled to overflowing
    my mother's pink and silver tea cup.
  Filled to overflowing, spilled in ever flowing compositions.
 Pooled, connected and strange
as common as unreality. As clear as
sage on the landscape
 everything growing – piñons, orchids, spruces, palms,
  water in channels inside and stored, clear.
  Take me with you, you growing flowing things.

Oh Cabezon
2001

Winter - Spring - Summer - Fall

Winter

PRAYERITIS

Grant me the serenity of an elevated noise
which is heard by no one but runs everything.

Grant me the peace that the security
of living in a posh prison brings.

from HEARTBEAT

All this power of the infinite moment
tells me:
I can *too* be a part.
Not apart, but belonging
    to the great heart.
Female-Male pairing of the universe.
Hear me by allowing me to listen.
Great heart beating, imparts
    the power in my chest
for me to do any damn good I'm going to do:
free me through the arch of my own work
to make more than money and not be a jerk.

COOLEST
(hearing Bird)
Skies open their hearts to the flash continents
jazz as only jazz is, jazz
repeats nothing, introduces something –
nothing is but something.
I found no pain in Charlie Parker's heart
    when his music lives in itself as lip heaven
and Bird's knowing world opens Spring,
lilt singing, crush heart improvise a lark –
flash around the world, continental drift
voices in cells freed. Voices unique tea.
Drinks shoot up stop. Hell stop.
Open surgery sugary torch, jungles burning.
Forever pure original song in the seed, tongue.
The flash of living Bird living won, one, among us.

SLOTH KILL

      How can out of chaos come chaos endlessly
without being reborn anew another thing?
    Stopped is trapped repeating old stories
        as stagnation sets in and I live in the past today.
    Prayers pray a way out, they tell me –
        I pray out of the hole I fell in, I stay there.
I put myself there and pray to get out fruitlessly.
I have to undo what I did endlessly.
    I don't know what to do, help me to focus,
work out of laziness, out of not working.
    The sloth eats me alive as I pray dying
      to change. How boring I am, Mr. Disorganization.
I want to die unrealized. Rubbish. I'm new, I hear
    something clear it away.
      Today, today, today and today.

OPEN TO

Bewitch me with possibilities.
Turn the corner where we can be free
to take the love potion of reality.
What is honesty but love
    in all its varieties?

EARTH LOVE

The summer of his love and frolicking in thick meadows.
The spring of his love to work it out
    chest to chest.
The fall play of lying quietly in the mountains of peace,
    the seasons of pleasure of the heart
    brotherly souls and love of one.
The friendship of the heart, fur and hand, explored in
    gratitude for the gift of his Earth.

MOON JUMP

Flowers in crevices budding out
as I follow where I flow, hot springs
bathed filled let out, passage of
    what was left from time.
From time to time now the full moon
    above and gravity down below
following my erotic erosion my
lifting of the spirits and release of tension
as a friend said, why do I see, like the Aztecs
a rabbit in the moon.
The moon jumps down at me as I am
    pleased to see it, so full of life here
so full of dawn, so full of mystery.

THE WELL OF TURQUOISE

On Circulation, on Flowers
on the ultimate dependence of Man on Woman
on the Earth Magnet, on Star Fires
on Water on the Earth and godly presence
    in the Spirits of Things
on the Overall and the Under-all, the Humor and
    the Love *above all and in all* –
the Love that flows things together
on Energy in it which is of it
which is the same thing at its best
the Energy of Love which makes things efficient
the Energy of a god's flow
    which you can never know
as you breathe it, as you are it
as you are me, and I nothing.
On everything, on the connectedness
on on and on off
the one-two character of the Universe
as it speaks to me on far on near
on yours, on mine
on the discovery of Imagination
    every minute of the day
Prayer as it breaks down rocks
    into good Earth
on Openness, on Honesty, on Willingness
    to listen, open to listen, truth in trust,
on the Blood's circulation, on the Heart's
    dependence on the Mind
the Mind's dependence on the Body
the body's dependence on
    growing good food –
on Killing with Prayer good meat and fowl and fish
the Game of Life which includes Death
death and the Beyond never known
    the Unknown –
Plants and Flowers and Seeds dependent
    on Water –

On water of everything, on scarcity and vision
the absolute dependence on water and air
the beauty of my love for you coming through,
on humility which is giving of myself without pay
on the "on thing" as I live it, on breath
on the organization in chaos
the circulation of the blood in the body
the body and the mind making things
    building a room, inhabiting it
praying together which is heightened discussion in it
on the embrace of man and woman
man and man, woman and woman
the embrace and love in every specific
the game of good and bad as
    I play it for the better
on the Elders of us leading back in wisdom
the acceptance of the Vision of the day
    as I hear it now –
on the embryo of hope I share with someone
the acceptance of faults that don't harm anyone
the changing which is growing
    which is conferring new things
        with those I love
which is connecting the spiritual with the actual
    until it is the same thing
on the teacher-student relationship which
    continually reverses
on getting damn good at what is done
    and therefore helping someone with it
    to come along
so that growth is the Energy of flow
the absolute dependence
    on everything I am given
every minute of every day
and this love for my Wife and my Son
    and the Daughter of the Universe as
        anyone can know it
on this continual reminding myself of
    surprise in being alive

as much I can, even in foul weather
    and the hardships of a cruel dawn
as everything balances
on the balance in now, in this,
on seeing, on those who can't see
on the privileged helping someone who has not,
the sick helping the sick into health
the specific of this line of thought
that emerges like a fountain in a rare Artesian well
well, on well, on water again
on recognizing my faults and taking
    action to make them better
removed or eased and handed over
on giving the problem away
by working in the enjoyment of now
    out of harm's way –
on our being together, what can I say
this giving of myself is all that I can say
our guidance as we work it out together
family and friendship, on love
ever on love, touching on love.

(from the waters, the clear Turquoise Well)

FLOWER

Dearest flower
perfumed in ecstasy
the tiniest hour
expanded into eternity.

SAM SCHWARTZ

Her father died and his tombstone lay on the
    ground above him keeping his spirit
from wriggling around.

MIND

I have no peace of mind.
I have no peace.
All I have
is mind.
Interrupted
displeased
confused
disoriented
unfocused
painful
useless
sidetracked
memory-filled
and hopeless
mind.
Mind.

TRUE SELF

There is a sense of the Great Spirit
    in every cell of my body
when I breathe in deeply inwardly completely
letting go slowly out, out.

When I breathe in deeply inwardly completely
      fully, hold–
and let go slowly out out out out.

WAITING AT BERNALILLO COUNTY DETENTION

probation
protection
procreation
procrastination
progress stagnation
predestination
appropriate nation
new notion
no recreation

uncreation
protection
protraction
emotion
reaction
probation
rotation
probation
/see p.17

Spring

IN SECRECY

Little did he know
I brushed my penis against his hairy snow.
The tender parts of my arms
against his bear charms,
the verbal ecstasy of his rough voice,
the muscular advance of his heart.
The winter of his retirement entered and kissed.
The rain of his lips and growth of his fur like
    the forest in mist.

WET BODY

Water continues to blaze trails
soft touch hand   hours enter canyons
lies on the bottom of everything
the feel crazy feeling that is the feeling of life
uninterrupted knows
the gentle hard path, the soft walking
brushing away the pebbles
hands leaving impressions in rocks. /21Mar

BEAST IN MAN

Beast in Man.
Man in Woman.
Woman in Beast.

BOWL

Nothing comes to me
fragments
of a falling God

am I falling with it
into the emptiness
of a bowl.

A LESSON IN LISTENING

If you listen you listen like ears.
You become ears and their innards.
You are hearing.
Every ear is turned on.
Focus comes naturally on the voice
that   like a blessing   urges expression –
the voice you are hearing
the words are urgent,
the sentences complete the sense.

The person is grateful you are hearing
that's the way I see it
cutting out everything else but what you're saying.
My talking becomes irrelevant for now.

You are opening up.
What a kiss in paradise,
the only solution to solitude's blues.
No matter what, I listen.
Every color becomes a part
of the clear picture I
am seeing through my ears.   /3Apr

TINY TINIES

What are the building blocks
of the building blocks?
    Tiny whizzing things.
What are the building blocks
of those?
    Energy is the sole foundation
of everything.
What are the building blocks
    of energy?
Tiny whizzing building blocks of things.
The soul is the foundation
    of everything –
whizzing building blocks of things.

THE TRUTH OF IT ALL

Unfortunate mesmerizing donuts
have led me all my life.
I've prayed to them, followed them
called them Val, called them Herbert
given them things, asked them to do things for me,
thought they did, cursed them when they didn't.

Unfortunate mesmerizing donuts
dancing away, powdered or not
entirely too sweet, entirely too demanding
leading me from day to day to nowhere
Val? Herbert?
unfortunate mesmerizing donuts.

SUNLIGHT LIGHT

Apprize me of thy being.
 Whether seeing, believing, achieving, receiving
  reentering from ceiling to floor
   kneeling or standing
   go out through the door
    into your outer being.
     Be mine, claim life and light.
      That you are there before me, *claim me.*
       That I am no more, no less, but
        what I hear in the space I open up
         through emptiness, for you to enter.

That direction given follows, follows leads.
 I follow with an open heart
  as the search apprizes me of your pulling strength.
   I don't look, don't hear, don't look for, don't hear out
    anything.
     But growth energizes the mind
      and the mind reflects the body
      and the body intertwines with
       the cosmos of causes
        and the universe of spirit
         which is dancing plus and minus through every

 Mirror of Delight
  that leads me on, awareness
   that leads me on to action.
   Action *with*, not action *on*,
    release of everything that goes faster than I know
    bigger than anything, smaller than creation
    all history now in the tiny speck I am
     bridges gaps and leaps to me
      one step at a time.
       Pulling pulling until I am embraced.
       Sunlight glorifies the morning ahead.

ALL I HAVE

Gay Byzantines build tessellated saints
in the church of my vision and
for that I am grateful, truly glowing
    blues and bright eyes and serene knowing
in the apse of the church,
Gay Byzantines' unknown flair for the eternal,
may you rest in peace while living, and after death,
always in the reflecting cathedral of my mind.

NO MYSTERY

My prayers are to the Great Unknown
 the Top Bone
  the Bottom Line –
   here is the bottom line:
    it is everywhere
threading through space
 and back again
  everything but me
   and in me
    all good and all things at once
the mystery paradise
 struck between the eyes
  in peace, in serenity
   if only in pieces
    calm, my little mind.
Out of the emptiness
 the greater emptiness
  filling up the cup
   of tea
    jasmine, fragrant, orient
     brings the world together:
      no mystery.

FREELY

In that chaos of the morning the night took over
and backwards time ran until it ran forward
and then stood still and the animals came out
and the flowers and bees consorted
and the great voice started up in the continuum
"Expect nothing and thou shalt be blessed."

    The humans who were new on the scene
        didn't listen
    until their hardships were so extreme
        it opened up their ears.
    Expect nothing and you will be blessed?
    Oh how can that be?
    Accept everything as what you see.
    Expect nothing and you will be free?

        I can't seem to let the grace flow
        the serenity of presence
        the *calm* that guides all power
            that is mine to claim
        and yet I analyze and trouble and pester
        and get myself into a tight impediment
        against the freedom to act
        the ease to energize
        the blessing of the commitment
        to follow through
        to the joy of some completion . . .

        Free me to open myself
        to you which is the empty me
        with open hands
        free to love who's in my presence.
        Free to give out all that you give me.

PLANTATION OF REAL

The mystery of the mastery is muddled in make believe
clearing out the garbage opens the ears –
I hear cars, starting up going, going, dogs barking
a motorcycle climbing at the slope of the hill.
I see the new house in our view, approaching it seems.
I see the blue sky and jumbled puffs of clouds.
Lifting fluffs of cottonwood, too early?
I care what I hear: the Tom turkey gobbling.
When am I going to do him in?
There's the dirt bike sound and the answering gobble.
And now a plane overhead, no, a helicopter.
    Looking for dope this early?
The plantations of reality set in.
I'm tired of trying to make more of it than there is.
It is impossible to continue to do this.
The past pity and future fake.
Now commands. Take the garbage of the past, the trash of the future
    to the dump.
I'm willingly mystified by the sun low in the sky
and the birds that repeat chirp chirp cheep cheep cheep cheep.
It's a texture of setting day, what is more to say
on this April 26th Two Thousand One.

MOOD ELEVATORS OF THE DHARMA

Mood elevators of the Dharma whose mysterious light lightens all,
that you're working ceaselessly to do your job is evident in
the darkness that glows as I turn the light out to discover you.
Discover, uncover, free, I turn the light back on, electricity flows in
the synapses of my brain and opens my touch with reality of the first
existence and the first, the last and the lasting. The evidence flows
through me as through everything. It all began when it began
without having to be created, spontaneous as the beginning of life
that required no antecedent, nothing before. It sprang into being and
is propelled propelled, now inertia in everything, the mystery
constantly unfolding in the ease of my presence of mind as I release
to your instruction the entire day, the entire night, the entire way.

TELL ME

Express yourself.
Tell me what you don't want to hear.
Break the rules. Tell me
what it's truly like. To listen to *me*.
I've been doing most of the talking.
Don't let me get away with it.
Harming others. Harming myself.
Dominating. Step back.
Take the ropes. Tell *me* to listen.
Why must my minutia storm you.
Rein me back to silence.
I want to hear silence.

What happened that led to *your* silence.
We share in our innermost selves
    together.
Talked out includes you.
Tell me where to listen. More
In the days of hours.
This infinite time of friendship
challenged to grow.
You tell me
what I don't need to know
what I don't want to hear.
I'm listening.
What you tell me
is like water.
Water of life only us desert dwellers
can appreciate.
It is as pure
as humility
truly to be experienced.
What you tell me
allows me to grow
in my desert. /9May

WILD HUNGARIANS

Wild Hungarians couldn't drag me to god
because when I got there I could only feel
the rustling of wings and the removal of pain
some friendly breeze came and it wasn't enough,
I could never evaluate the concordance of
    evolution, the birth of life progressant,
        and all the other intermingled and interdependent
            stages on which this instant of life danced –
in short I took it for granted and it was granted and
    it was up to me to see how free I was
        appreciatively
to now bless where I was dragged by
the wild anythings
blessed by living it, aware, will I
appreciate it more when I'm gone
no now when I can and do, got up
to piss to wash my hands drink some
cherry lime orange juice chew
some vitamin C put
my glasses on, go out naked
and see the stars and clouds
and birth of the moon
to remind me what grace is all about
free and on the table.
As I lie back down and the dog
rubs his eyes with his paws,
discovery: thank you
for dragging me here, whoever you are.

THE HAPPY POULTRY CLUB

    The Happy Poultry Club is happy to offer our first-time sale of
Professor Outright Slimedick's delightful 154 lecture series
"How to Be a Financial Winner by Pushing Poetry in your Face."
For the next 24 hours this course is just $499.95, $200 off list.
    Highlights?

1. Poets Buggered in the Renaissance.
2. Skirtless Transgendered Disclosures that will lead you to fame and fortune.
3. How to write fast-selling sonnets that make more money than commercials.
4. Alcoholic misfit poets that will help you rhyme your way to wealth.
5. Poets who dropped soap in the Dark Ages.
6. Wealthy Gizzards who sold so much poetry they now own the banks.
7. Computer wizard poets who have bought up Silicon Valley.
8. How to write from madness, dyslexia, and misery, those best selling epics that everybody loves.
9. Homeless poets who've become business tycoons.
10. Poets buggered in Kansas.
11. Poets buggered by tomato worms.
12. Straight poets I have known.

A PIECE OF YOUR PEACE OF MIND

Can you recognize peace of mind?
15 minutes ago I recognized I recognized it.
I did experience it or thought I did.
    Uh oh, there it is again
that right now of a moment ago.
If I think about time passing
as it's constantly changing into the now disappearing
    I go crazy and give up.
This moment encompasses everything
as so many have said better than me.
If I'm a poet, sing about other things.
The classical music from the other room,
The pre-dawn blessing of being with my family in
    separate rooms in this house.
Even the dog curled up sleeping on his bed
    next to my bed.
My wife's showering, the new kitty meowing,
my son drawing, in a rare moment of peace.

ENTRANCED

Everything is entranced in the estrangement of the dance
where leads follow the abrupt romance.
Surprise flies in the face of misery
and all washes away that was dirtied and delayed.
Freshness starts up from some untold place
that becomes familiar as an old book
old sage or something new again.

Nothing has been written from this dance of nature
yellowed Jonathan apple leaves
nice green apple leaves on the younger tree.
The green with many suspended cylindrical cones
of the upright spruce, our solstice tree of old.
The pushing out white groups of roses *blanc double.*
The green of the grape vines with baby, baby grapes.

The untimely reddening of the cherries on the tree
bit by borers
The tanager with bright yellow breast
topping the neighbor's far apple tree
the hardened off tomatoes in four packs
left over from the garden plantings
to give away – Sweet Million and Early Pick
from old seeds
the farther near sloping swelling breast of
the hill we see North of us
piñon covered, dead grass covered gentle
arroyo drains on its side sloping out and down.
Oh perfect virgin, as the houses build up your side
human status the conqueror and the rapist.

Oh this dance, the freshness of this weekly irrigated nature
zebra grass, 2 feet tall already, rhubarb, wild anise
apples cherries apricots some peaches
and lots of almonds, some black berries
and black raspberries
coarse screech of scrub jay
at the pear tree's base.

Dance dance dance all rooted to the ground
 and flying species,
   and noisy crickets and village dogs barking, stopped
    as the undefined, unwritten dance continues on
     to freshen my standing here, my reception to it
       my participation by giving in to it.
        How unknown how undefined how unwritable
       how rare and how immediately obtainable
      by not seeking but by
    entering in to the movement.

   Movement in growth, as the ancient eroded mesas
        in the distance sloping to Jemez
   and geological archaeological finds continue.
Immersed in it, take me away from human form
all plants garden trees living flying sounding forms swallow me
into your everything and free me of this guilt
      of my human downfallings
   free me as you are doing, as you, the dance of the Creator
     creates endlessly in life sap and exchange and change
       beauty, as if I don't exist.

THE JOY OF REJECTING

"It's time to Christianize the pulpit
turn everything into what I am
which is On the Cross 24 Hours a Day
bleeding profusely, suffering suffering
till the day I die.
I do not exist but I can be dragged out
to frighten you
by evil anal bastards
until you *rebel* and reclaim the joy
of rejecting."

HEAD OVER HEELS

My head is head over heels
and cracked brains with Creator
freeform lightly devilishly heavy
as includes everything
every dark corner is lit up.
Praise fallows, praise fields
praise the heart of the constructive mind.
Show the way, Mirth,
that we can understand in love,
flip flop over in light-heartedness.
The dark cover is ripped off
as the false shroud it is.
The real dark is illuminated
with the beginning of everything –
that orgasm without foreplay
that started all life,
galaxies that can collide with galaxies
without stars touching.
The dance of two in one and one become two.
Billions and billions of stars in our galaxy
and so far apart
brings me back to Earth, to dawn, to day,
to now the 1st of June
irrigation day, when most of the trees are full of fruit.
When everything is energy and I need help to move.
Brainstorming with the best
my body comes to life,
as Venus disappears into planet day.
Love take me where you go
always there whether seen or not or thought of.
Goddess of love leads my heart in the art of
life in the waking moment
the morning of new reality returns
disappearing love, always there
to guide me through the working day.

AFTER SUNS

Sunset of my heart
 afterglow of burnt orange in my blood
  nipple of the world in my eyes
   focal point of everything –
    Cabezon, volcanic core old as surface earth
     right where the sun goes down around the solstice.
     Here I am asking a connection
      to pull me out of the grave I'm in
       where I buried myself with my own indecision
      my wasting time away in laziness
     in the ability to respond to high Art
     and low Earth calling.
    Let me be free with you, after sunset
   to die with me into another night
  to rise with me into another day
 when I might set things right
and forgive myself for too much forgiveness
and in turn act, do, focus one thing at a time
 up the ladder to your heart.
  After you Sir and Madam of the Earth,
   afterglow still, in sinking.

FLOWER AGAIN

Dearest flower of the universe
unfold
unfold
bold.
Gold anthers touched by
the stuff of the Gods.

FACE IN MY FOOD

Does anybody far North complain
ruptured star in the main
about the spaghetti of Turin
where crop circles are on the brain?
And paranormal nights broadcast
frequencies of uptight.
Oh worry about the massive change
that is cancer on the brain
where the future furiously reconsiders
what it ever was.
    Does each instant of our past
    have to be regurgitated?
    Is the dream of over the rainbow
    simply a bathroom noise?
Oh where is what and how come who?
Who came, who cared, who carried the weight of centuries?
Where are we going up against *what*?
Don't read too much from the Bible, Westerners.
Don't sit too long in thoughtless thought, Easterners.
And those in the middle, watch out
when you lose your focus.
What's saying to me from the broadcast frequency
X E L E N T, all night mastery
from the deserts of the distant past
and sunlight of the future
lights up wild green plums
and newly booming *spuria* like
tall skinny iris, bronze and gold tipped.
Give everything up to the risk of knowing nothing
and nothing knows you're coming
and dresses up to be something
to be more than something
to be everything
    and why not go out and play whether it's recess or not?
You're not in school, nor am I,
this is life.
"Read the signs or listen to the tapes
if you can't read,"
the voice from the desert speaks to me
out of the night.

You don't know nuthin' but ego,
human ego, ego, egg on your face
face in your plate
passed out from too much drinking.

Wake up! It's headache time.
Nauseous stomach.
Weakness of mind. What mind.
Oh maybe if I sober up I will reach
    the sublime.
Is that now, as no pieces fit together?
Or do they.
What do I know, Joe Blow. Harold Insignificant.
What is my real name.
Baby Larry, just born.
Just reaching clarity of the mind.
Starting his own radio station
Mesa Mountain Network.
Oh infant noise. Coos and burps.
The miracle of insignificance.

CRUSHING EGO WARS

The Full Moon follows where I syncopate
    its instant heartbeat
it's path and mine joined in fluid pounding.
Oh investigation of all ruins on the moon
we are connected as we fly through sky
    gravity high.
Where did all the man-made hatred come from
    more and more and more
fighting over lessening space, our egos huge, dominant,
wanting what we've always been given
    when Nature was Queen.
Now the Full Moon is, dominant over our species.
Sailing pure as it ever was
as we argue over fewer spoils
in our crushing ego wars.

BETWEEN US SINGS

Sacred texts displayed before me:
"I come down to be the Wind.
I come down to be the end
that flows into beginning.
 Before you know it,
 know it.
 Go
with me down the canyons
through the cactus needles
across soft flesh.
 Be with me in the dawn-sunset
 of the mind body passages of
 fields burning, flowing
with water.
 With water, come sacred down.
 Sacred being being is-ing
 is is as is is.
 Two things seeing one another
  that's all it ever is.
  You, me – the wind, the breeze the zephyr flow
  between us
is equaling as,
 is outdoing us as
 greater flows of stars in
 a Milky Way
 fling our spirits out.
  Don't ever say we are alone
  in this sacred text of dawning
  sunset spread out constellations
  of the heart,
   constellations of the heart
   yours and mine mingling
   in ever love.
    Sacred means sacks of red blood flowing.
     The wind the backing, the gentling touching
     as all turns out into darkness, the night
     that is the sunlight of the mind
     sunlight of the spirit sight,
      seeing anything between us

absolute trust
heart to heart
the wind silent sings in the souls
 of our one
 our one destroying lonely –
 our friendship dancer
 our lover pleasure
  our spirits knowing.
  Two coyotes lopping down and
  off to the arroyo
  where the giant cottonwoods
  root up to the sky.
  Me and you flowing
   leaves high,
   summer at peak.
  Night high
  as the peep of dawn
   as the middle of anything
   where we are fixed together
   simultaneous rocking
   like talking back and forth
    back and forth
    and now together
    the words before me
    what you say I do
     in the marriage of spirit and flesh.
     The friendship which is our togetherness
     even when apart
     none in the spirit of the night.
      What words talk.
      Yours to me
      as precious as the free
      talked out
       commitment that is
       what it is
       a continuing bond
       of give and take
       freely given
       totally taken.
        Breeze
         easily

                free
                caresses
                  holds
                  without touching
                  we are together
                  forever touched out.
                     Discovered in passionate souls.
                     Speaking to you
                     or are you
                     speaking to me?
           Unknowingly, now knows
           everything.
           In love, the human spirit dances.
           Now knowing
           a little
           of a lot
           between us.
           The pure bell rings out to silence
           above my front door
           hello hello.
      Hello
hello.

TOUCHED

Mountains are flowing where the rivers are going
no place but where they've never been.

Whether they're there or not if you look and don't see them
don't ask where they've been.

They've never been anyplace if you don't see them
unless you're not looking when they're there.

Where are they? Are you looking? There. There.

LISTENING LOVE

Sky powers, ornate desires.
I love you with love that even love loves
that sent you to me, to my heart.

Unfolds reality, Aphrodite and
the arrow sent
more like a waterfall, a torrent, tornado
the aftermath of having been blown about
drenched to the dry bone
with desire. *Everything turns on love.*
It goes out, grasping and wishing
as you haven't the slightest idea.
I'm at your command, General
where do you stand? Away from me.
The heartache is pure. The dish of reality.
I eat nothing from the plate.
But I hear every nuance of every word
you say when you commit to me
your thoughts, infinite details of your life
put together the picture.
I'm just the good guy as long as I listen.
And my urge to have more than that
to have everything but not letting on
keeps my ears open, at least
keeps me in warm affection.
Stunned as I am, when you are close to me
I play the friend well, in fact I am.
Perhaps the best I can be.

PRECIOUS WISDOM

The sky is the limit.
I play my cow kazoo.
The birds practice wisdom
and sing back
choruses of old.

BREEZE SPEAKS

The cool breeze lifts the curtain at my nighttime
    bedroom window
and brushes my shoulder.
The wind increasingly comes to listen to my self-pity.
Or rather I don't know what it does but blow
and touch me at reminder moments.
"I am here, cool, knowing, as, from place to place
I cross over you. Poorwill in the distance.
Night commands. You get hold of yourself.
Claim strength. You have it.
Fire your bad workers, they don't work for you anyway.
    (anger, impatience, laziness)
no one tells me what to do.
Go back to sleep is common sense
    at 2 o'clock in the morning.
Play for yourself your breathing instrument."

I hear music, at last.
Insistent at my elbow, my past.
"Strike up to the present.
Lead that orchestra
back to good nutrition
and fun in the ocean
even if it's the ocean of your imagination."
My imagination, my ocean.
My companion
Wind brushing my chest.
There's always someone here with me
whether I accept it or not.
I feel it the wind the music the coyotes
the dogs
the birds, the crickets
the refrigerator's ice maker –

6000 chemicals have been added to the food.
How about pure water now.
Tea in the morning.
Dreams perhaps remembered, tonight.

OVER POP STRANGLEHOLD

One hundred years of Danish Picassos
is enough to freeze ice over Hell
and then the imitation Rachmaninoffs
paraded their infancy.
Life is an annoyance when there's nothing authentic.
When having tea at four requires
using the same old tea bag
until there's nothing but the hot hard water
you started out with.
What more can a bored month of Sundays do
    but rebel?
Why did Mozart have to die so young of supposedly
eating uncooked pork?
Good God, give us genius
back where it belongs
in the right place at the right time.
And enough of these watered down nothings
that come out of our own stupid
overpopulation.

WHAT EVER HAPPENED TO
FINE THANKS?

Hi Joe howr' you?
Ecstatically fabulous on a plane where nobody else is.
*And how are **you**?*
Oh I'm okay, thanks.
Gee that's great. Well it's just amazing to run into you.
Yeah, good to see ya.
Have a stupendously great day, enjoy.
Yeah, see ya, Joe . . .

HAPPINESS IS A THRILL NEVER KNOWN BY GOD

(Song)

Happiness is a thrill never known by God
as in his severe throne he sits on a thorn.
    I fly over here and find a good life
    where sunlight begins to boost the light.
I joke with that guy in that throne overhead –
will I see your truth only when I am dead?
    He slaps me with dawn and I laugh when it's day
    even if I feel bad and don't do what I say.
I see your descendants on Earth all around
and in stars and the life force and love in this town.
    But you've got such a groan in that throne overhead
    why don't you just go to your angelic bed?
We'll take over here in Mother's sphere
take your long rest, Daddy, you have nothing to fear

Summer

I AM NATURE

Lubra Picasso
lump lump social status
he was the first ear on the block of thumbs

Does it have to be a clear message
in order to be a clear message?
"I spake spoke"
I stayed spoke
I spoke spaken
I specked spoke
I stuck speak
I speak take
take speech for instance.

Why don't you simply take speech
and start from there.
Start over starting anything.
Having started startle.
Naturally
I'm a found nature.
I am nature
Nature and I are more than buddies:
We are a mature *one*.
We are in recovery together
following the same path.

We are one.
You asked for a voice here is a voice.
Human Nature is just one of many natures.
Nature is bigger than human nature.
                              (put on "Nature" mask)
"I am nature.
You, you silly thing
are just human nature.
Human nature indeed.
Look what you're doing.
There are too many of you it's
as simple as that.
Did you think the planet would get bigger
as you grew in numbers?
I am nature. I don't need to get bigger.
Nature spoke nature.
Kick your ego in the butt,
stop killing other species.
So you invented toilet paper
and you invented the toilet
so what?

Where does it all go?
Now you want to extend your billions of lives.
Now you want to turn into billions
of robots clanking around
stomping the Earth flat.

Have fun, idiot, worshiping your ego
and applying the latest salve to your soul.
Your soul has a hole in it.
And the only thing that will fill that up
is Nature, not human Nature.
But us.
Yes us.
The natural sunset of us.
The earth rise of us.
The universal kick back of creation.
The evolution of us all of us.
The wonder of you doing nothing
and looking out   at us
living out our lives in equal opportunity.
Us trees gardens the precious canopy.
Destroy us and you have destroyed yourself.

Lubra Picasso.
Genius of laughter
Mozart of the soul.
Duende of the spirit.

Make yourself whole.
You murderer
you opposite of Mother.
Murder.
Your greed and ego and self worship,
self-justification
justifies your murder of other species
other life.
Shakespeare gives us words
to write your stupid tragedy.
'Lord, what fools these mortals be.'
Which is not without
comic relief."   *(take off "Nature" mask)*

DRUG

That damn caffeine
kept me wet and dripping
when I should be dry
a fly on the wall of eternity
all eyes,
waiting to be swatted.

DISCOURSE WHILE EATING GARDEN SALSA

Most meditation in America is run by the human ego
telling us how remarkable we are
rather than how destructive
except for those individuals who dedicate themselves
to the frequencies of Buddhism
like Joanne Kyger for whom
the light of the West Coast is necessary
for seeing the past, present and future in the now.

I've eaten that before
somewhere in the mixed up past –
it is a familiar ride of constant daily discovery.

LOVE APPEARS

Love appears
   when you let it
when you keep coming around
   the same person
and your lives intertwine
   it takes time
but love appears to stay
   when you let it.
And you two are blessed by it
   all the way through.

ARE YOU A BODHISATTVA?

Are you a Bodhisattva?
 Are you a buddy satori?
  Satori is when you get hip with a vision
      in light of the world.
    You get it, they tell me. I just pass things on.
    And when you get the message "hang up"
      Ram Dass says.
        Now, what is my spiritual name
        if I fit into any of this.
        Brother Half Eye Open?
        Brother Small Vision:
      Oh I just saw the world, blink,
      I lost it. But I remember it.
    What did you see?
    I don't see what you see
   Or do I?
  My name is To Aim Right
 to go in an orderly direction
one foot before another
without harming any other soul.
I saw this morning
 when I went outside East
  there was Venus prominent
   in the pre-dawn sky.
    Are you dreaming remembering
     another dawn light?
      My name is small potatoes
       Just a cog in the cog of the wheel.
      Wake up and understand
      if only a little.
     Wake up and understand
     wake up and know love
    and you're a bodhisattva
they tell me.

EXOTIC ENCHANTRESS

Echo indifference tower flower
never too late to contemplate
what does it all mean, no answer
but in the asking of it curious
man woman child especially
baby, why do we dry up most of us later?
I don't, won't, can't, everything is endlessly
calling calling me to investigate, I am
an investigative reporter with little time left over
from routine clean the kitchen clean up
cook, take garbage, feed pets fix
kitchen faucet, go through mountains of chaos books
life falling out, tapes magazines papers
past surprises, things unread, thousands call me
find me out, "Why haven't you opened my book
you ignorant fool how could you," nose in the sky
pass me by, how curious, my grandmother was always
curious about every endless thing till she died in
her sleep, yes, it's possible
yes, up there on top of that tower in the sky
is the flower of Parasdise blooming that
doesn't pass me by. I see it differently
every time the fragrance fills the greenhouse
and the echoes of the tropical night open
in the photograph of the most exquisite, delicate
enchantress aroma white multi-calling
jungle canopy exotic bloom, don't ever stop
even after you close in the morning you
race the sun as it comes up the
blessings of the sunset, in the sunrise in the
center of my soul wherever whatever that is, it
is blooming inside me renewing interest in
everything. What was that you said?

MORNING TEA

Hearts of flowers, fresh routines –
whether of breathing or listening
to the flower-faced hummingbirds.
When you leave I'll be without you, little pals
    that I have sat by with your whistling
and whirring all summer.
I can still breathe and naturally seek flowers –
the sunflowers now and the wild little
portulaca, morning glories and a single red
    dahlia in a pot
I can move in when the first of winter comes.
Why not be poetic when you enjoy life so much
or be a poet, forget the *"ic."*

Poetry should be free.
Anyone who takes money for it should be reminded
how freely it was given
and is, all the time.
Contests are bad for the blood of the poet,
unhealthy as jobs teaching poetry
unless you are open and free and organize
readings for your students and
get them to make their own books
and publish them themselves.
Yes it is a self-sufficient gift.
As is these morning flowers I have my tea with
    every *morning*,
as repetitious as Venus and Jupiter and Saturn
preceding the dawn, it seems all summer,
as I get up to pray and start my day.

Poetry is not competition or you turn into a
    barnyard rooster distorting your voice
crowing and strutting away your life
no matter what sex,
all sounding the same
no one is to blame.
It is time to rise for the morning surprise.

What is that you say,
    Flame on the stove?
"Give me a pot of water to boil
    to make your tea.
Meditate a little
    not too much or you'll get
carried away with nothingness
and get nothing done."
Let the barking dog in,
feed the meowing cat
make strong coffee and rye toast for my wife.

Venus, perfect where you are
you are the morning star,
now lost in the dawn
as the day is coming on.

HEAVENLY BLUE

          Dearest flower
            swirling up in the dawn of discovery
        of the truth of ignorance –
     out of the shock of the depths of pain
  comes you
morning glory
the innocence of the daily reprieve
    peace in calamity believe-it-or-not beauty
       fragrance even in this miracle of life
         the permission of everything
           to do the best it can
            after all.
         What species are you
       precious dawn flower of light
     earthia spiritus particular eye
   a light blue within without
breathe in and out in discovery.

NEW BREATH

The tearest tore tore. The terrorist tore.
The terrorist tore hate. Hate tore
Tore through everything – evening
morning sun. Mourning.

Tore his heart out. Tore out everyone's heart.
Tore out pre-columbian American no-name no god
    heart out lifted it toward the Sun
American Earth Mother tore out her heart
where there was no sun lifted it burn out
lifted it American Mother Earth tore out her heart
lifted it her breasts forever divided
tore out her heart lifted it to
the burnt out sun
hate of the angry too late feared too late to listen
tore out everyone's heart in the morning lack of sun
hate young sons in the pit of anger
tore tear tore out everyone with it
everyone who was there was everywhere
where their source was the loneliness of despair
working together as a determined sacrifice to hate.
"We give up to you Hate our lives too late.
Take everyone down to ground with it
my hate takes your fear down
my isolation in the past too late."

    Tear tore
hate young sons in the pit of anger
from the pages of fear and tear everything apart
tore my heart out threw it down to the ground
for the world to fall on.
Out of this we listen as we fall.
Open our hearts that are left to listen or we fall
all the way around the talking circle of the Earth
to shut up and listen or we fall.

Listen to the anger playing itself out
from the heart of the cult of hate
the sacrifice of the cult of hate
those of us who are not too late
listen to the anger playing itself out
and then, maybe, it can be of help –
the compassion of love no tear no tear
nothing torn
is the breathing in and out which continues.
The anger playing itself out, breathing out
the compassion of love breathing itself in
and out. As I listen
the compassion of love breathing in and out.

DOWN THE DRAIN, A HOLY BOOK

    Book the One, Book the Two
    Book the Three, Four
   Sailing through the door to eternity.
   The giving of face to fodder
  Flash to fortune
  Jewels of Heaven taking care of you.
 After death real life continues on.
Those left living continue consciously.
Consciousness is eternal as life.
Life which sees itself, the world
is the miracle, the intertwining of necessity produces
mutates a grace, a gift which sees itself.

Book the One, Book the Two
Book Three.
 The beauty of the world just
  had to be seen
   to be believed.
    What you do with it is at your disposal.
    Written on the tablets of foam.
    Pushing through those doors
   the floors open
   ceilings kiss my feet
  I am elevated. I am humbled.
  Just looking out the window to a rock wall
 is a prayer.
 That is breath. Feathers. Turquoise from Nepal.
Quartz from here on a hike in Placitas.
Can the dead direct?
Can the living command?
No.
Only the giving over in substance, all substance I can know.
In this breath deeply in and then out
as the single bell sound dissipates.
And the sun knowing everything, proud of our planet
    rises.
Can we be humble enough to love?

Fall

OH WHEN I DIE

When the last pear has fallen
and my heart is stopped
who will conduct the donkey serenade?
Who will lead jackasses on parade?

THE ART OF LIFE

Open my heart and allow the art of life to display itself.
If Earth isn't art what is it?
Canvas laid out in a globe with
Picassos in every inch of Nature –
Dekoonings Pollacks Rothkos and Redons
in patterns where I look
as the seasons change. O'Keefe and Arthur Dove
as Goyas present the panoply of people
and Gertrude Stein reads to us in the waves
coming in at the edge of the ocean.
All the great art is an expression of the Earth
in inestimable beauty or gratitude toward
the Creator of the heart, the mind of everything
the feeling of great, as the tragedies and comedies
of the art of Earth speak through the hands of
    Shakespeare into the art of now.
Every pain, every celebration every common work hour
the art and expression of it all, lives, rocks and dances.
Is its own in its own fresh music, bright reflection.

GOODBYE

Our cherry tree the borers got
looks wintry this September
but is dead to the core.

TRUE LOVE

Flower of onion wealth
give me the tomato kiss my beet heart deserves.
Never does the sky open inveterate monsters
without turning inward to surprise.
Nature is All and All is nature
of which Man is a tiny part of Woman.
And she and he are but a single species.
Be warned. Be firm. Be true.
Be open to the meditative spirit
which kills your dominating atom,
your meditative spirit when the bell rings
and any other time, breathe in and out
and know it is better to observe than conquer.
True action follows the meditative nothingness
where everything takes over
and I am but a tiny vital part.
What do I know, the eternal question asks
which takes greater energy, breathing in or out?
The more I give to Nature the less I know.
I give up my baseball bat and stop
beating life to a pulp.
The garden accepts my kitchen waste
eventually everything breaks down.
Break with it. The joy of observing.
This is my final act. My prelude
to garden onions, tomatoes, orange bell-peppers
jalapeños, grapes, pluots, green beans.
banana squash plants the size of elephants.
What isn't beautiful? But it takes work.
After true pause. The bell ringing
in my irrigated heart.

MORMON

Pristine picture of hog-tied heaven
where everything requires endless dusting.

SOLAR HEAT

How poetry flows out of nowhere into somewhere.
It's like a temperature control.
When things get too cold
something happens to click on
 to make things warmer.
  And it doesn't just happen in language
   it happens in sound
    all around.
     Do you feel the warmth flowing in?
     Listen to the bell.
      Are you breathing deeper?
      Are you well?
       All those people who need it
        who don't have it.
         Or don't want it.
          Don't see it.
          Don't hear it.
          Don't feel it.
            When the hole that is empty in their soul
            won't fill up.
             Won't overflow.
              A giant click
               and the sun is on.
                Warmth flows in
                 through the windows
                  the floors
                   the heart of the mind
                  when poetry is
                  what it is.
                Peace of mind
               of a most
              curious kind.
              A disturbance in the soul
              which urges growth
              and a constant
              revelation of enjoyment.
              Pass it on.
              Oh human
              basking in the miraculously
              clicked on light.

ANTHRAX AVENUE

        Ann tacky tacks
        commingle your double
        time in despair pair off
        sex creates fun
        fun creates parties
        parties create alcohol
        alcohol creates dope
        women create men
men create half a dozen killing enterprises
        made in New Mexico
        tragedy crosses the border
        everything gets reversed
        in the car of the future
        the home of the triple car garage
        the spoiled brat of the past produces
        spores of unbreathable future
        time travels backward and ends in
        the Pope's lap   the Poet's rap.
    Anthrax Avenue ends
    where the Batmobile dead-ends
    and has the last laugh in Carlsbad
where the radioactive wastes burp and throw up
        hungover from a national binge.
    We dropped our guard now everybody
    hates our backyard.
    That's what you get for sucking the sucker
        of secrecy.
    Trying forever to pull the wool over
        the sheep's eyes.
We are the fat lambs led to slaughter
by a government that doesn't know where it's going
except to the decimation of the universe.
namely the best of all countries eliminating nature
a one species world, namely ours,
with robot greenhouses and cattle ranches
roaches and ants and aphids we try to murder.
Yes the problem is a preponderance of egos.
Human humans that are not too human.
We've made lots of progress the "we" tells me from the pulpit

and yet it's true: Mozart, Anna and the King of Siam
Mahatma Gandhi, Buddha, love and compassion
   yes, tolerance.
   Tolerance and democracy.
   Back to the Earth, my only home
   as I return home.
   Home again away from home.
   That home of hate is not my home
   but a fundamental cult
   of backended young male assholes.
   Breathe deeply. Garden
   and practice husbandry
   follow the stars.
   Act like you got sense.
   Disorganize.
      Follow your dream if that includes
      the world of Jane Goodall
      Woody Guthrie, the great cathedrals
      and the kivas
      the natural order of recovery
      day by day
      from the drunken disaster of greed
building houses so big no chicken would live in them
      light lightly.
   Here with humility to shape me
   if I let it.
   Let it out
   in the music of communicated life
   to the jazz beat of the heart
   the hearing of the soul
   the giant helping of helping others
   for dessert.

AND WE THOUGHT GERTRUDE STEIN WAS REPETITIOUS

   Retaliation is a retaliation of a retaliation
   of a retaliation of a retaliation.

A BIT OF PEACE

      Wait until the inspired moment
      presents itself.
      When is that?
      When there is a why.
    Questions present themselves in the answers.
    Answers whirl forever in their place
    on mountaintops in my mind
    slightly outside my mind.
    It is a miracle I can see outside myself
    let alone think.
    Think broadly or narrowly
    preferably open mindedly.
What is why and how.
How is. It takes work to figure it out –
long hours of experimentation that may lead to nothing.
You have to beat the bushes until there is nothing
let alone fire.
    And then a rabbit jumps out.
    Or when I least expect it,
    I jump out.
    A presence says "Hello.
    Get down on your knees and give thanks.
    What are you doing down on your knees?"
    Giving thanks.
        "Why are you giving thanks."
        Because I don't understand anything
        and I'm still alive.
        I'm more than alive.
            Do I deserve it?
        Shame turns to guilt and I can
        ask for forgiveness.
        Rug, forgive me for walking on you.
        Particles in the air, forgive me
        for breathing you.
        Wife, forgive me for
        robbing you of a life.
    Son, forgive me for
    putting you on the wrong path.
    Or do I presume too much.
    I do and I do and I do do do.

And now I'm married to the true self within myself.
The true self within my mind.
It is a difficult relationship
but productive.   Why?
Because I don't ask, or try not to.
Clarity pokes its funny face at me.
    "You write too much.
    You say too much.
    You interfere with the gift."
    It says to me.
    "Simply breathe more
    and talk less.
    And enter
    a new found peace.
    Please enter
    a new found place.
    A bit of peace   is okay."
    Breathe deeply says the master
    the mistress
    the mobster
    when you escape the danger.
    Breathe deeply.
    A bit of peace
    is okay.

LIVING IN THE PROBLEM

I'm totally lost.
There's too much information.
I'm killed by it.
I don't know which way to turn.
But look up the answer
to this problem
but whatever I find
is just more
information.

UNCHAINED MELODY

The weeks go by
like flying debris.

Time only stands still
on television.

The harsh flow of beauty
stupefies
here while there
the horror   piles up.

It's all in the mix
the good and the bad
gyrating into one
awful thing.

Too many of us and we become
like ants, like aphids
destroying the plant,
for us, the planet, we are on.
Destroying each other
under any guise
of death-god.

Give us release
peace.

May the source of this
misery see
the gift of love
tolerance for others
compassion –
the permission of peace.

May the bombers
only bomb
without exception
the idiocy of hate,
the cult of human idolatry

and the suicidal madness of
retaliation:

let there be an endless chain
of education
equality of living things

that the criminals
may be brought to court
and receive due
justice.

POWERLESS AND FREE

With money comes power
with power comes the energy to deceive
to perpetuate the be*he*moth:
therefore keep me small.
There is no human power
except through false pretenses –
the planet which was here before us
is our teacher and guide
if I'm small enough to listen.

The human ego is a false god
whether I like it or not
but now
I'm forced to see the truth
admit reality
as ego which is death
stares me in the face.

EMPTINESS IS NOT ENOUGH

Emptiness is a concept
I can't grasp.
Every time I read it
my mind draws a blank
which is anything but empty.
I'm sorry, oh Eastern wisdom
the word does not translate –
what does it mean?

But don't try to explain –
all the explanations in English
add to the problem
instead of taking away
where I can see clearly
nothing exists.

EL MALPAIS

Oh old awe full flow
wander where water would go.
                              low cccc

Lava up from below
red in molten show.
                              low cccc

Dried till black cracked
million years el malpais
                              up to eeeee

oh old awe flow
badlands where water would go
                              up to gggg

dried black cracked eerie
spread farther-than-the eyes see.
                              back to cccc
            (sing in exaggerated monotone)

SOBER BARTENDER

He is the binding force between the odd and the indifferent. If he's a built-in part of the brain I want to know how and why and what does that mean. I'm an analytical pragmatist though I'm not good at either. I do know when to give up pestering a problem.

    I sing from the bar rails. My bartender provides me with incredibly exotic drinks. Hawaiian Punch Sunset Surprise. Dawn Equilibrium Open Door Fizz. Now is the Never You Thought Was Going to Happen. Uncertainty Delight! My Buddy's abundant arms shove toward me the drink of Air, the breath of Fall, sun coming up, the metallic blue hoist of Heaven on Earth, the reentering the surprise of the Sexual Union of East and West. Some children will be from the West, some from the East, some a mixture of both. We talk about it, my bartender and I, as the goodies keep coming – the unexpected delivery from his abundant hands, his warmth listening to me as I say nothing. He says nothing but I listen and he keeps me drinking in the air – the growing brilliant sunrise right out my window and above the rock wall. I drink in everything you give me, you great big fantasy buddy. You are so real I believe you as the gifts keep coming. I have no tab here, only the friendly bar of reality. Sometimes it sucks out there, but here, the drinks of the real keep coming, the sun so bright it stuns my eyes. And I breathe in sounds and light and red cherry leaves in this rising Autumn, this day to end all days. Dying into its instant birth, changing, brightening. The sun ultimately up and me back home safe in bed.

PRACTICE

    Practice
    where thoughts interrupt
    a vacuum meditation.

    I am empty space
    full of stars.
    Empty space.

LAST PLAY

My last words
last words
at last, words.
Words tell the story
of the storyteller.
None of my stories
have a plot.
The only character
is my mind and body
and the spirit
hovering between.
Spirit is an implant
that dissolves into
reality.
Suddenly
there's a play
there is a play
of characters
the director
is real
if only we
could meet.
Coyote
Mother Nature
Wife
Son
Father
of my heart
Mother
of my life.
The play
plays on
till the end.
Why bother
with a rerun?
There're so many
fresh dramas
right now.

RIDDLE

Is he dead? Is he a floral membrane?
Is he vast and articulate? Is he
consistently negative? Or the opposite?
Or all opposites? Is he indigent and creepy.
Is he beauty all over and in-between?
Is he in full command or the supreme Egotist?
Is he the cream of the crop?
The cream of all crops? Is he a she? A flower?
Everything? Does he bear speaking of?
Is he barren and pathetic? Does he read?
Does he combat the Pope? Is he just is?
My buddy? My budding flower? In November.
In this coming hour. Is he the glue
that makes all glue work? Is he pregnant? →

Oh he must be the Empress with Child.
Does she abort the child? What is her attitude?
What connects connections if it is not she, he?
Space and marrow of the atom,
oh everything in this tiny space of my head.
Oh the unalterable urge of the imagination.
Is she alive? Is he alive?
The biggest word in the English language is truth.

BREATH, FEATHER, FRESH AIR

Meditation of the breath.
Is the breath itself meditation
as it is airing through the nostrils
whirling into the lungs fresh
and arriving out in air expired
just blended in with the day
or night vapors.

Oh breath, in and out
what are you thinking about?
As you pick up oxygen
and deliver it to the greedy lungs.
Thank you, I say to you
whether you think or not.
You can be without us
but we wouldn't be without you.
Breath, feather, fresh air, breeze.
What do you think
about us?

from THE DIRECTION OF ONE

Go out to the fragrant breeze
that is large deep red apples
I picked up and put
in a plastic bucket
yes
I'm gathering   and the mask I made
the end of   of Nature
the season   as I want
as I turn around   to personify
to the hill North   everything
and the oily rototiller   and to the East
and stack of cut   the reflection of
fruit wood   white buildings and beyond
drying   the tip of
from the dying   Cabezon
cherry tree.   and mesas
And to the west the spruce   descending
rises   and above
into the blue sky   is what
and wash   pulls me down
of watercolor clouds   below
and to the South   to be who I am –
the door   nothing
to the portal   no one
and reflection   not here
of blue clouds   I'm just creating
reality by
perceiving
in my own mind
as I cease
to exist.

IN MY JUNGLE HOME

The ding-dong pussy from abracadabra.
The kangaroo cock from Kalamazoo.
The lovely love birds from Love Canal.
The turbo-jet from the Isle of Blue.

All come together in the Island breezes
tropical seduction of the fantasy resort
Tropicana mug-wump dancing bananas
Prancing rooms in the hot-tub cavort.

Cool off papa, mama enough
mama and mama, touch and tough.
We touch the tenderness which we sleep
in the world where real life leaps.

Nirvana Satori, the apple of your dreams
is the exotic fruit of your heart.
Lie down to pray any day any night
anytime the sunlight hits the mark

the curtains close, love alone
becomes the wildest jungle home.

IS IT TRUE?

Prayer is exciting the air with your thoughts –
silence is an ear full.

START OFF

    Here ye, here ye
        you hear?
    I promulgate a new era
    everyday
    every minute
    right now
    peaceful here
    morning on my face.

  Go get milk for tea and cereal
  shout at the dog "Stop pestering the cat!"
  Breathe deeply in and out.
  A raga for morning begins –
  slowly a beating appreciation
  of unwinding dawn unwound.
  A sound of a Japanese bell I ring
  right now
  disasters, I shake you off.
  I'm breathing, I'm alone.
  I put one foot before the other
  walk now, walking
  regenerates the heart.

I'm bipedal.
My musculoskeletal system
needs excitation,
rejuvenation of my
orientation in
3-dimensional space.
My proprioceptors
in my muscles
in my tendons
in my joints
want to be informed
of where my body is in space
as I walk along.

My cerebellum
is excited
coordinating my locomotion
and
my muscles.
Oh right leg and left arm
cross-patterned,
oh left leg and right arm movement
generating electrical
stuff in the brain
harmonizing as I walk
my entire central nervous system.

Thank you Dr. Weil
for telling me this.
Exercise supreme.
I thought it was so simple
but it's really music,
a neurological symphony
of my own sort –
visual tactile stimulation
as I move along.

Oh let me
walk my talk as well as
talk my walk –
path of light discovery
come what may.
Walk it out this morning
through anything
by everything.
Into it all I proceed
simply, simply?
Putting one foot before
another.

CLICHE EXPLODED

The last leaf on the poplar tree
    is it clinging
    in the breeze
or wanting to be free –
    or is it
    just there
thought-less-ly?

AT LAST

I went to the holiest of the holies
the most sacred of all that is sacred
and there on the altar of altars
right before me   was
(breathe deeply in and out)

MORNING, DAY AFTER THANKSGIVING

The flower of light opens
where last discovered.
I light a stick of incense
and pretend
I have its presence
like all those who tell me
they love this delicate spiritual essence
this glow
that maintains such power
this more than anything
this more than a flower.
No word is enough.
I'm permanently lost
in pretense.
But go on and
sit, enjoy the incense.
Breathe it in with the air
my life depends on.

DANCE SLOWLY

Detect it all
in a fragment of holy writ.
Writ out, who writ it out and from what.
From who, inside, outside himself
    to say:
"Dance slowly
don't become an artificial vibrator
and don't
ever listen to anyone who says *don't*.
Unless it's to keep
your hand off the hot stove
for the second time."

And that's where the text ends.
I followed and found
in my spiral-bound notebook
drifting from God knows where
on the page.

LONELY

We have been lonely
too long –
let us be lonely together.

RESULT OF MEDITATION

Wow what happened to my ego?
The world thunders in.
And now everything is quiet.
What a relief.
The music of nature takes over.
What a better boss.

I SHOT CLARITY

The post-pituitary pop-tarts of the paternalistic generation
have been amalgamized by the milk-toast contingent
of strong-arm surprise: Yes every duidairy
must have a slip-grease transmission lockup
where oozing grease begins to be a problem
in the back-firing departments of English and Sewage.

Therefore literature on the toes of the Century disappearing
has turned into vocal noise where individual voices are
blended into a structural stew which
stands on its own two feet and gives in to nothing
and bores the Century of the past
and now is decomposing in the landfill of tomorrow.

Thus ultimately the fuckhead can't write and
should be demoted from the ranks of the gun-shy.

I *shot* the writer to put an end to his
endless spewing, gushing out of dated vacuum tubing.
Clarity should ever be sought out and killed
as I, post-structural pachyderm of the
world's most prestigious toilet on the hill
universe buttress on the Upside-Down University
of publish-puberty-or-perish, have markedly done.

I shot Clarity long ago
and now put an immediate end
to my crack-pot grunge-brain colleague
and acanemic tenure-robbing competitor, Finis Penis.

Please pin a butt-plug to my lapel. And I thank you, fellow
death of language splices and multi-conglomerate
    fart police in the Academy of Just Bad Shit.

        Your President,
        Turgid Thunder Mug,
        Piled Higher in PHD's than you'll ever know.

Breath
2002

∽

RED DUST

A spaceship takes me up
from where I sit,
transports me to the Mars
of Oblivion
where I see
a thousand red seas
all parting for my little toe
to pass.
There little toes are infrequent and worshiped
by the Mars Oblivions.
I'm in luck and I have two.
The planet's in ecstasy –
my presence has blessed their history.
Red bells ring, the face in the landscape speaks
"Oh thank you dear Earthling
for presenting us with your little toe nail clippings
we'll keep to remind us
of miracles."
I was transported back
little
toenails clipped.
Oh benevolent Martian Oblivians
how can I tell the truth
and be believed?
Your admiring me
so went to my head
I forgot to grab a little red dust.

SUCH AS IT IS
for Steve and Jane Sprague

Everything is exquisite
as the Ponce de Leon find,
the fountain of youth flows
in the passing moment.
Eternity is always youthful
as it begins always from the beginning
as I do, no matter
what age I am.
No past no future
not even a now.
Just is-ness, such is such
a gift giving away,
a moment being momentous.
What now.
Tired from
the first day of a New Year.

Posole
biscochitos
anasazi beans
homegrown poblano chile
jalapeño relish and flour tortillas
pistachios
apple juice
tea, coffee, local bing cherry wine
brownies baked
on sour cherries,
olive bread friends brought,
homegrown almonds,
a tap dance on the kitchen floor
all after a late morning hike
to the Spring
and up across arroyos
to snow patched hills
overlooking the houses, the Village
and down here home,
warm with
the closest of friends
blends into never-never land
reality plus reflection. →

January first
bursting
with pleasure.

LONELINESS LIT UP

      I am a tool of Nature
       That I do know
        I get my commands
        from outside my window
         where breezes blow the dead grass
        where the cherry twigs are covered
       with buds waiting for the Spring
       here now in cold January sun
      out bright.
       What do I know?
      The light illuminates my brain.
     I see sparks along
    dark passages.
     I see rocks stacked in a wall
    and an elk horn.
    I see that God is a light
   and doesn't bear speaking of
  as I see it in a raven gliding
  through the air
 and disappearing.
I know you are there.
This is where everything is
that teaches me,
out the window,
 where peace is   inwardly
  along the corridors
    and millions of years of evolution
    to this moment.
     The sun lights up
    the hairs on my arm
   and now the loneliness
 at least   is
at peace with itself.

CONFESSION CONFUSION

I am white.
Does that mean I'll fight?
Does that mean I'll rape
and take
and break?
Does that mean I'm loud
and aggressive?
Does that mean I'm rich?
That everything I touch turns to gold?
Does that mean
I'm Christian?
I'm big and perfumy?
That I'm a twig?
That I take LSD
and stomp on canaries?
    That I
    am a bloated Sphinx?
    That my gut's burnt out?
    That I drink alcohol from beer cans?
    From vodka bottles?
    From milady's slipper?
    Does it mean I'm contrary?
    Hate natives and play with fairies?
    Does that mean I lack all color?
    That I'm a business man
    with a business head?
        That I'm a doctor
        a lawyer
        a gynecologist?
        a real estate developer?
        an egghead?
        a dead head?
        a non-head?
        a red-head
        a big head
        a flat head
        a cop?

Does it mean I created a war and asked you to fight it?
Does it mean I have a culture
that isn't worldly?
That I can never never play jazz?
That I grew up in a vacuum
and terrorized a city.
Does that mean
I'm too big for my britches?
Does that mean
I ask too many questions
am incapable of love?
That my Mozart & Shakespeare were barking up the wrong tree?
That the tree that grows out of my ass should be pruned?
That I'm deviant
that I'm male
that I'm full of kingfish
and rainbow bread?
Eat steak and potatoes
and worship Barbie dolls?
Does it mean anything?
Yes, yes,
all of the above.

UNCONSCIOUS SONNET

Higher than fire beyond which everything depends
Hangs that which is unchangeable
A vision to the end
Everyone clings to as it is changing changing changing
Unknown, unknowable the mystery deepens
Under each star in every galaxy in every way
Words are unknowable for it, till it disappears,
And out it comes, released forever never to be the same –
Constituent atoms, oxygen and breath
Warmth of the body, heart of the hearts
Passing frequencies, coming into focus
With the light turned on, the cat on the banister,
    Shared air, bond, compassion for the living
    Burns into action, as I start over again.

STEPS

1 I really fucked up
2 and now I'm crazy.
3 I've got to get on some spiritual path
4 by writing down my wrongs
5 and then tell them to someone.
6 I've got to get rid of these
7 so I'll ask for them to be removed.
8 I'll make a list of those I've harmed
9 and make amends to them.
10 I've got to take care of my problems everyday
11 and expand my life through thinking about it and prayer
12 and actually, at best, help somebody else.

GUIDE

Heavens
mystery of all my fears
underneath my star cap
I tilt my head back and
gaze straight up into the Zenith
my head visualizes, beyond grasp
beyond skull, beyond mind.
Unknown Star at the top of the universe
the cold envelops and reassures to the bone
I hurry in to the fire and enormous burning log.
But that high star or was it planet was it
other planet's burning Sun, forever too distant
unknown worlds, gazes perhaps more knowledgeable
than mine, a sure thing that, *guide me* I say over and over
the top of the universe could be the bottom bottom
and get shining at top height knowing past autumn, the winter light.

IN MEDIAS RES
for Hepzibah Stein and Ezra Nebuchadnezzar

Had I the energy of the Tao I'd form battalions of peaceful nitwits
    I'd enter the dharma of the heavenly Earth
    the endpoint of Katharine's girth
    the hippopotamus of children's turf.
If I plowed the sewing kit of a dangerous birth, I'd hope
    the carillons would ring till the Christians lurch
    and Easter stuffs its Christmas back into dirt
    and the pagan pussies unite to a dickless first
    and the monkeys embrace to evolve a human thirst
    for love and laughter, wouldn't you know it, wouldn't you
    throw it out of meditation, as everything
    comes back in with a cement truck flattening
    my brain out from man to woman.
As I get up in the middle of the night and place the exercise mat
    on the flagstones in the middle of the living room floor
    and do a standing slowly turning around run
    with my arms stretched out as I turn
    running in place, it is my own little helpful dance
    for my bones and the blood running through my veins
    which is the only reason I'm sane enough
    to be open to some change.
    Axis. Thomás. Influenza.
    A pin. A pat. A pew.

CLOSER

    I'm closer to Whitman than I ever thought
    not to his greatness
    but to the arms of his soul,
    the soul being the great awakening
    of spiritual energy.
    What little I can know of a piece
    of the Great Spirit
    charged with love in the embrace
    oh! the embrace.

EULALIA HOPE

The Flapjaws will stop flapping when you get your
    head on backwards.
    Oh loony loony loony loony loo.
    Oh pickle pickle pickle pickle pick.
Sky opens margins to unearth cows.
Too many four-footed, not enough one-footed.
    Oh wrinkle wrinkle wrinkle in the ink.
    Oh spittle spattle dattle why not think.
Oh owing. Oo-ing oo-oo, Ahing ah-ah
ah choo choo choo   sneeze backwards   I have no head
I've been destroyed by hope.

I'm Hope. I'm the femme fatale and
    wouldn't you know it
the man, mean Al.

I'm Al. I mean *Al*. I blink and
that cow goes back to a whisky wink.
I forgot I winked.

Hope: You winked at me and stuck your foot out.
    I almost tripped, but I gave you Hope
    at the end of your rope.

Al: I don't need Hope. Hope ruined my dope.
    I may be a dope but I don't need Hope.
    Oh fickle fickle wouldn't you elope?
    Oh piddle piddle piddle on your soap.

The cow. The murderous cow.
The body. Where is the body.
The booty, who got away with
the booty?

I am a soap opera singer. My name is Eulalia Hope
I sing Maudlin Tuesdays and Hamburger Wednesdays.
I'm the big ass tank-sized fly in the old ointment.
I'm Al the Pal who drinks so much he lost the gal.
I'm the stumbling block that don't know any better.
But I'm not bitter. I *am* better.

Oh Al. King Al. There you go not remembering your nose.
Does your nose know. Do you know any no's?
No. No. No.

    Oh fiddle fiddle fiddle while it burns.
    Destroy destroy destroy the evidence.
Where is the body left by the murderous cow.
    Oh I'm the body body body bod.
    We're dead and dead and dead that's why we're odd.

And I'm the cow that did the dusty deed.
I trampled on the chorus of the moon.
I got so big so many of me
I got too heavy to predict.
I took over and everyone singing on Earth got sick.

    Oh sicky sicky sicky sick it sucks
    but that's why I'm a charismatic duck.
    Oh quacky quacky quacky now I'm dead.
    We're all in this together in this bed.

The worms are dancing end on end.
And all the one-foot limber pogo sticks
are hopping about, full of hope.
Yes I am Eulalia Hope and I come about once a year
hoping, don't you get it, that Al will surprise
and open his eyes.

I'm Al. Your pal. Don't cow-tow to the Moon.
There are two moons anyhow.
Pardon me while I pass out now.

    Let's forget forget forgotten Al.
    Eulalia you'd better catch the cow.

You've caught yourself. You've done the deed.
You're so many you're heavy in greed.

    Oh greedy greedy greedy greedy cows.
    You got so big you trampled me and how.
    I can singy singy sing one more
    and then I'll be forever out the door. →

I woke up and caught that cow.
I got hope and gave up dope.
Let's go Eulalia, Eulalia Hope.

Well, Al. You threw in the towel.
We might have a margin of error together.
I'll stick around and we'll share new ground.

    Oh singy singy singy singy sing.
    This is my last song and the sing is sung.

Eulalia Eulalia Eulalia Hope.
We don't need so many cows and all that dope.
I'm happy with you as the sun comes up.
Oh Al as the sun goes down, I'll still be around
I'll still be around.

SAD STORY

Life is an art as the early Earthlings found out
God hollering at them,
"Hey you! Lift that potato peel, smooth out
    that onion skin.
Overlay that vermillion with orange.
Keep everything Natural. Grow Organics.
Be beautiful in young old age and I'll give you
    old age.
Age agelessly, darling. I love you say to me,
    as I love you."
God stopped hollering. The cats and dogs took over.
Life stood in the way of life. Life took over.
The Spirit waned, eking out a poor existence.
Religion took over and ate just about everything up.
Monsters yakked at each other how each other's clan
    was better.
Hell was invented and you better believe it.
What an awful time. I cry as I write this.
Oh God what happened? Your Mate, Earth, is dying.
Sorry, I can't continue.

FISH STORY

Healthy Water from Noah's Ark.
    How do you know that?
Well it's labeled.
    Do you believe that?
It tastes good.
    When were you on Noah's Ark?
Last night. I picked up this bottle.
It wasn't the only one I drank.
    How was Noah?
Fine.
    And his wife?
Fine.
    And all the animals?
I didn't see any.
    What were they doing, Noah and his wife?
They were cooking stool pigeons.
I don't' know where they got them.
    That's impossible.
So is everything.
    No it isn't.
    How can you cook a stool pigeon?
You go find one and cook it.
They were labeled before they took the label off.
They cooked them in bat guano.
    No wonder you took the water and ran.
Ran right out of that dream.
And all I've got to show for it
is a drink of good clear water.
    That's remarkable.
Isn't it.
How possible everything is, especially in words.
My real name is Fishface Pablinsky.
Here have some.
    What?
Healthy Water from Noah's Ark.

THE GREATEST STORY ON EARTH

The story of everything I've ever been told.
I was born in a cocoon in a little log cabin
    on the stream of history.
My Daddy was a Farmer. My Mother was an Elk.
I was brought up on porridge soup
and they put lace on my panties attached to my Jockey shorts.
After I reached public display my brothers and sisters
    abandoned me.
I was put on a rubber boat on the Nile and
ended up floating down the Mississippi till
I came ashore on an asphalt highway.
After getting drunk across the country I was arrested
    thrown in jail where I
wrote the Greatest Story on Earth.
It started with prophets prophesying that they were prophets.
It ended where it started except Science was invented.
Then came the Crashing Ear Horn and Gonzo Republic.
Earth split in two and became a Quack Master.
They put me in the hospital and robbed me of my voices.
I was forced into a 13 step program and
    came to believe I was the only power I had
and I was okay, so you better get your act together.
Now I'm cured of everything but drunkenness
    possible addiction, and flaming uncontrollably.
But I douse myself out and become sane again.
I married for the third time and passed away in the
    arms of my first child.*
What he will think of this I'll never know
    but the truth never hurt anybody.

*His name was Dwayne, son of my first wife, Eve Arden.

FAMOUS QUOTE

"What do you expect from so many gurus
but hypoglycemia,
multi various egomania
and ill-fitting bras."

IN ONE PLACE

You can do it, hey, say
Life is beautiful, except for the atrocities.
If one of those don't get you
you're home free
to work and play like a good boy.
Speaking to myself, visions of
mangled words or a stir crazy soup
of alphabet noise.
Note, freeform, silence is music
the Twentieth Century, with Duchamp and Kandinsky.
I've come into contact with too much:
that's the blame, never enough, the game
    of real reason.
I can't see too much good art, great art
can't even get to it.
Having past, it adds up.

What is he saying? Life in
its tragedies, it's seeming
enjoyment, it's pure contentment
don't forget the laughter, can't
get enough of it or art, especially
Great Laughter:
it's okay, *more than that*
it's all I've got, or did have.

I have a nice fire going in the old tarnished
    iron stove.
This place is clean, and relatively
spare, for glutted us, and
    except for the atrocities
which nobody can explain, let alone
God, it's
as fine as it
gets.

BRILLIANT END

Silicon Dogs.
Rushed to Limbaugh fanatics.
Pants with your pants down
Everything's exposed.
Triple by-pass toccata.
Fugue and furor in the sixth tense.
Everything takes on a peculiar sense of love and composure.
Now that I look, actuality presents itself.
Reality emerges out of yet more reality.
The afterglow is burnt orange.
The spruce tree and bare apple tree are silhouettes
against it.
Everything is part of it, going down
to come up again.

SHOCK TALK

I'm going to do what I'm going to do
for a hole in the wall is hell on wheels.
I poked through with a dime splatterer
coin-operated words:
it cost me considerable to be free
to hear at anytime a new species.
Qwawk-talk.
What are you tarking to me?
The valve canals are open.
Oh Reverah, Reverah, we are as close as close can be.
Where is the Sterling Sea?
What happened to the Past?
How many years have we been married to bowls of cereal?
Who came through the hole in the wall?
A New Century Cast of Characters.
Real people, at last.
All the pieces came together.

The elixir fairy darted back and forth with
sparkles dancing.

PRE-DAWN DANCE

The Cosmos dancing in my mind
 like whirls of pleasure in the evidence of their glowing
  seen, having seen, been, having been
  whirls of stars in the bursting pleasure of themselves.
  Sigh through space, a slow, slow breath
  invigorates the Cosmos, passes through
 connects the God-Body to the God-Brain
 the thinking through all of everything –
 larger than spirit, dancing ever outward
from the original Kiss of Creation
the deep entering space connection
the explosion of *realization*
 the true self of Stars, of Planets of knowing
  of creatures forever viewing the last glimmering sunsets
   the sleep of Death
    and the first evidence of the first Breath of Life
     the predawn Dawn
      the reassurance of the Dance
       that unites the Day.
        Oh come what may
          up.
         Oh come what may.

CHARM

I was wearing charm after charm after charm, trying to reach
the pinnacle of time, handmade black cloth with scenes of
harvest swimming around a farm house, some bright shirt and
striped pants, necklaces and feathers, and when it came time to
swim, everyone took off their clothes to dip in the creek. I had to
take all that off. She said to me, "All that magic has to come off."

TALK

Talk is cheap
unless you mean what you say
and then it's priceless.

BAD DAY

The resentments that pickle the Universe
come in, come out, come where?
In the Giant Kitchen of the Gross Imagination
the cook and the cook-etes
pour that vinegar water and the pickling spices
into vast tubs where stars galaxies and planets
black holes and asteroids flirt with each other
gravitationally
and as the vinegar pickles everything everything
turns dark.
Resentments hang like darkly illuminated curtains
throughout the cosmos
and the cooks are pleased:
they've turned everything *sour for today.*

GOOD DAY

Now someone got up and took a deep breath
and everything lifted
resentments fell like hair off a rat
and gloom dissipated in far corners of the Universe
    as well as
the mysterious Center nobody knows.
You see, it wasn't a matter of control
it wasn't a matter of anything but
the connection of someone's mind and body
as the spirit of breath infused, allowed
to come back to life, life
and the dawn was reminded-of-its dependence on the sun
and the sun bonded with the dawn
    and the sky and the reason why,
everything was what it was and continues to be free.

HAIRNET

"Interbeing endlessly interwoven"
Interbeing endlessly there,
there where the here is, here-there
I connect by way of a connection
to a connection there, where
in a roundabout way we are connected.
Connected, connected, whole, here there.
What is the word other than
everywhere. How can I be everywhere?
No, I'm here-there. I'm thither, thither and about.
About to be there where I am.
I'm just a hairnet in my Mamaw's hair.
Somewhere there I am. On that net.
Forever connected.

THINKING STRAIGHT

Twelve-forty and the clock strikes odd
in the ganglia of night.
The planet is always bathed in light
somewhere morning,
noon and night.
How dark it is on this side
why of the why of the why.
Stars fulfill sleeping pleasures.
It is the gift of knowing how to live
in the quest of it all –
darkness bathed in light
it can't even see
and vice versa.
The opposite of pleasure
is pleasure
one measure at a time –
a bit of the old sublime. /5Apr

IN THE CALM
at Hummingbird Camp, Jemez Springs, NM

Our Father and Old Woman fits us to the wind
on the high mountain.
 The wind sings devastation to the Twins
  the Twins of the sky, the Twins of the Earth
   as inter-relations enter relationships
   enter the phase of the new becoming.
    New relationships, new becoming
    Sober to the pure Earth pounding.

   The heart, heart of the night, heart of the night
   macho dissolved in the dawn
   false strength gravitated to the pounding
   and now beating of Earth –
Earth birth Earth Magic in itself own self
be pure, in listening, approaching,
the faint burbling of the stream
you go a long way to get to,
  you go a long way to get to anyplace near.
  Anyplace near the stream
   as I sit down listening.

(Jemez)

   Jemez, Jemez Creek,
    To my left higher from a distant higher mountain place
    the stream now so near rushing thundering hitting rocks
    flowing at my feet, around and over rocks
   pool bed rushing by me, to my right, lower below
   the water of your miracle of the interpersonal
sustenance of the Earth, Earth light, Earth life,
the rushing of the water by me from my up left
to my right and lower winding out of sight away
 rushing, rushing water rushing from my left way out
  up there, now front of me and off beautiful clear
  changing rushing as I sit, to my right rushing off
   lower down to my right and away somewhere
   as I sit, entering the inter-personal relationship
   of the Earth, Jemez River, water, water –
   my connection to all things rushing by in the now
   in the serene now mysterious, takes me with it.

   From the wind of the Woman who spoke to the Twins
on the pounding Mountain, told them to find me
as they did in my little way in my two-part entity
 rushing left to right and finding myself
 in the now in this stream in the Jemez Mountains
  the Jemez Creek rushing by
  in the completeness of the two-part
   energy of the Earth, the Woman of the Wind
  to the Twins, to me to all to any,
  the freedom of being in a relationship
  with the teller, the told her, the tell it to each other,
 the one on one relationship with the Earth, Earth Baby
 stream streaming by in my mind still
in meditation relationship with my past
my mother my father my wife my new brothers
 sisters in the streaming stream, as pure as clear can be
 as it is now, in new relationship, in new touching
  on this pounding Earth turning free in this
  stream of constant memory, let go with it
   flowing by, calm, right in front of me –

                                                                     (Placitas)

Oso Spring bubbling up pooling out in the stream
 that irrigates *our* new spring garden of
new peas carrots spinach lettuce in the ground –
the water of the other spring brings me this clear mug
of water I drink in the middle of the night
all the way from mountain and my new
 relation, the power entity of my family –
Mountain Woman Wind pounding Twins hearing one to one
 one to two one to one in our inter relation
 interrelationship with this known Earth, the *stream*

   at my feet, rushing from left, to right   *(Jemez)*
   like a gale, but a river, whoever you are of
  the Earth and breaking sky, trees and identify
  with your rushing by, clear contentment that I am
  here, taking it all in, in, in   *(quicker)*
 as far as I can be from anywhere near
hear hear hear, here,
as far as I can be I am here
 no out or in, near or far, beyond or bypass →

no circumvention but streaming rushing by
from left to right do I hear
in this clear stream of the creek of the water in the Village,
 I see myself most clearly
with it in closest relationship turned into one
 to be free, see, I sit, here, to be free, sit, I see here
 in the calm between left and right
 clear as I can be. /17Mar

JUST IS

Always with me is the energy of an eternal life
but to tap into it, hold onto it freeing me
is the dream of a lifetime realized
or just flow with while I can.
Remarkable as the plain source is
I am blind to it, worried, bothered away
till I gather the pool sources, deepen
my breathing, stop, still, catch on again.

You're on for the ride, buster, star dust, romantic
dissenter, flavorer, taster of choice
master, mistress of surrender, defeated by all odds
give in to the strength imponderable, unboundable
just a release of grace of goodness that the Earth exists
alive in the knowing all things intersperse,
and share the power of reverse.
/20 March, Spring, for Lenore

CREATION PLUS

Bigger than God is reality.
It is God's master
a willing slave to love.

SOMETHING WAS INSPIRING

Something was inspiring
    lifting up the heart and letting the soul in.
The soul is a piece of God
    as I understand him
and I don't understand anything at all
    except wherein I am.
The more I am in my own skin
    the more soul I have,
the great mystery solved by just
    being alive being here
just now in this near-zero cold weather
without a trace of snow,
the fire burning a leftover
block of construction wood
and a piece of pine from up North.
    I toast on one side,
listen to the dog eating,
sip my Yorkshire tea
a little bit of milk and sugar
that stirs the soul up
as the blue of the pre-dawn sky
outlines the piñon and juniper scattered hill
outside my window,
my bare feet on the orangish flagstones,
the fan silently whipping the air overhead.
    This is March beginning
    in my consciousness.
The tapestry of giving
    what was given to me.
There is *no* wealth in my non-monetary soul,
    only the sharing
with no one but this moment of now
in the space of breathing.

AMERICAN PORTRAIT

I forget the furor of statisticians.
When I told this fellow that statistics lie
he shot a hole in my argument when he showed me
thousands of my purchases
traced to my social security number and credit card
and bank and check and shopping card numbers.
There was the thorough history of my life of purchases.

"What you buy makes the person what he is
and you are an atypical overeducated male consumer
but we've got a market for you and you can be sold
to the appropriate big business, any business
if it is a business is big.
Thus your junk mail and e-mail spam or even
newspaper inserts and telemarketing is your portrait –
end of story."

NO STRINGS ATTACHED

As time flies
fly time as a kite
and let it go.

SECRET OF LIFE

Next to where I peed
the pool sinks to
a waterlily in paradise
floating in beautiful
peachy dawn lake
open and fragrant forever
roots kissing the mud.

WE'RE INNOCENT

Everything is old-fashioned if you get modern enough.
    What century am I in anyway?
All the best was in that century I *was* in before
    overpopulation got us, got us down screaming –

"We are innocent! The human race never did anything wrong
except kill a few people. Just let us reproduce ourselves
and clone ourselves into perpetuity, eternity isn't enough for us
we want marching hordes OF US
over the planet over the seas and out into space.
We're innocent! Look at all our courses of self-improvement.
Narrow focus is our God who looks exactly like
    you and me!"

TO THE OLD POPE REFUSING RETIREMENT

    True, Christ did not get down off the cross,
        but he wasn't eighty-two!

INTERRELATION

    Give me a frond of a fern to learn from
        to go back in time to
    Goddess of the mossy locks
        and the morning dew.

LITERAL

    My eyes have lifted, mingling with the stars.
    It looks kind of funny looking out there
    at them looking back at me.

WHAT THE HECK

Poetry never earned me a Master's.
How would it? How should it?
Now what am I, a wannabe?
There is no substitute for hard decent work
sustained until the goal is reached.
I'm lacking there, using fear as an excuse.
I've always tried to be smarter than I am.
Ooh! That smarts. Self-analysis just
confuses me. There is part of the brain
I just can't put a finger on, the poetry part.
I'm not a poet, *per se,* but I have an open heart.
What does that mean these days. You're right,
poetry never earned me a Master's Degree.
So what good is it for petty me.

FIRST

Heaven of no known territory
Earth my only depository
Reveal all and I would be fixed
for the future.
For now, I'm a tiny focus
in the mayhem of where I am.
Clutter rules my life
no escape, no giving in.
No path but where I've been
leading up to the impossible.
And yet I have another cup of tea
and the aroma of sweet lilac
from the blue vase on this one spare table
begins to correct me
and pull me back to what is first.

FOR MY CLOSEST

     Think of me as your body
think of me as the circus of your mind
  the circuits of everywhere,
      the thoughts inflamed by passion
   of a lover.
      That you and I are entwined
    that is our reality.
      There is almost always more to love
  than people are willing to admit
or release, or give.
      Think of me as not everywhere
   but focused on ourselves to live open
in true love.

∽

COMPANION

You can't see inside the heaven of my hell
but I can, and it's a pleasant place
that doesn't start with "h" or end with "n"–
it has no name even when you name it
and now it enters my mind and begins to
    take over body–
I could get used to this place and live here
pleasantly in a constant air, but I give in
to other things, I know from experience.
For there is that hell out there, the living
pain and addiction to ghosts and false realities,
but for now I am where I could be more,
where perhaps things were meant to be.
Join me if you wish, it's an invitation.

DEATH SPURT

Over-popufandulation
over stick in the concrete ovation
over big hip in big kid kid a nation
over puppy pop a kill nature station
kill over spill all poison sex and infatuation
over sprawl all kill all farms, rub out degradation
million baby over old folks by billion squat on
    big fat crowd out dirt and crops just
        sprawl elbow to elbow Walmart fuck-ation
Fucked by too many man tooty screwed by ego fruity human
    stuck on one another no room for eagles or salmon
        corn or homemade handmade anything frozen
            micro waved zapped by too many zaps
                by too many of each other in each other's way
                in other words nothing but noise TV
                crowds people stuck up
                nature's ass
                    to kill it –
kill all but us top of the line one species conquers all
we are it hot shit on top of hot shit on too much
too many refuse to admit we've fucked ourselves
out of existence overpop-you-pew you poop you me you
stupid poop head dead fuck death ejaculation.

IS ISIS ISIS

    Bring into the present time
    the present time.
    Noumena, nominal
    now.
    Now in which everything is created
    for the first time,
    now in which the true self
    is.
    I hear the wind outside
    the cat moving on the rug and purring
    the clock's second hand clicking.

RIGHT ON

No matter what, it is a knot:
I'm married to reality.
What is escape anyway
but delay?
To accept erases the pain
to reject adds to the blame.
As I sail on in to the interconnection
the good with the good
the bad with the bad
the good with the bad
the bad with the better.
Better watch out feeling everything –
it's an adventure,
this gift of the boat of discovery
on the ocean of desert waves –
imagination is the real lilacs
so sweet you can smell them from
the other room.
It is the same thing
good or bad, what matters is
I am present and not
screwed up
with my head on backwards.

JAZZ SET ME FREE

Jazz oh be what it used to be
to set me free to
what is is.
I remember
what it is
let that be
to set me free.
What it is is
what it was
to set me free.

FIRST BREATH

There were falling curtains.
There was a death row additive.
There was being human
which was not often humane.
There was a list of all the wrong things.
There was opening up to wind
     which was harsh and rattled things.
Then suddenly there was a bell
rung clearly until the sound fell –
and in that he took a breath
and was reborn
returned to the baby of creation.

MUTUAL

Every word grounded
in my soul
by soul I mean
the breath of spirit –
it is the same
my connection with
the space I am in.

How can that be?
Honestly.
A bit of wind say
remember after I am dead
I did breathe in
the restorative air
of this planet
we share.
What can we care more for
than the air of the words
I put together to say
or hear
what you tell me.

ONE ON ONE

        Oh one wonderful   one on and on
          won not so one   not so one wonderful
one won one wonderful   on and on
              one wonder   one won one
                 won one   on and on
            one won one   one not so one
     one on one wonderful   on and on
            one won on   one wonderful
          one one won on   on and on
           one wonderful   oh one wonderful
             on one one   one and one
           on one one on   one won on
           one wonderful   and on wonderful
        one on one and on   won and on
        and one wonderful   one wonderful
                on and on   one on one
                not so one   one wonderful
   wonderful not so one   one on.

PRAY, THAT IS TO SAY

Prayer is an affair of the fair heart –
   we knelt down equally holding hands
and asked from the broken center
   be mended, grace of healing love.

And it happened over time
   the sublime was rendered casually.
It could be the only prayer
   is to ask what should be done
and the only feeling is gratitude
   for being shown the way.

PROFIT

                Over con consummation
             over suck up sumption
            over-consummating consumption
          how long are we going to continue
        over tintinnabulation
         over ten ten sump sump my gump!
         Over ten sum ate con some pump shoe shun
      over comp over buy over why over
    never do anything but too much gunk funk
and stunk thunking, over blab world.

          How much longer do we think we can over
                  rat's ass perfume?
    Smelling the garbage pit of front yards
                    waiting to be hauled off to the dump
   pleasant vistas of new real estate realities
         what a pleasant place to live and bring your children
up chuck where the shopping is near or far
and the shitting is in four bathrooms for two
                    no tea but coffee and vodka for three
and a wine cellar with *Vas Deferens* albums..

           What a beautiful place to buy near
                 and far as you spurt out plastic
  and investments of super-galactic eternities
      of corporate wisdom where Kings lead
               the moneyed takeover of Earth.
Be part of it, buy here buy there buy
    every product known to man and put it
in your own Museum run by your clone,
            the Herbert R. Kochberry Extravaganza
  Theme Park and Products-Up-the-Ass Memorial *Palace*
        with 4 swimming pools full of crystal clear filtered
  stolen water.
         And in every nick and cranny everything ever bought
by a man anywhere Memorialized enshrined
   your furs, your splendor, your tropical woods and mansion junk
                    and across the street

   your wife the Honorable Ms. Miss Muffet Kochberry
                    has on equally fine real-estate erected
 a lavish suite of gorgeous apparel rooms
     full of every product ever purchased by the hand of woman.
  Oh buy until you fill the sky with your mansions on Earth
          and there isn't any dirt left, *how long are we going to*
       continue to support the suspenders of the jock strap corporate?
  Ha! Over-consummation, buy the whole thing UP and
               sell it for a profit to the first alien retired CEO
from that faraway planet that has so much wealth
     he can retire there, this poor putrid scared scarred barren
                 ball of the former Earth we leave behind.
  Oh Ode. Oh over. God of the Freaks of Wealth.

                             ✦

A JAPANESE SENSIBILITY

       I put things where
         they belong
       and in that song sing
      leader of Paradise everything
          in its place
      a rare face on reality
    or is this what is really real.
   Might as well enjoy the irises
   and fragrant roses in the vases
        while I can
  I worked hard enough to achieve
  this sparse Japanese sensibility
   too many cows, too many possessions
   too many things, too many twos.
    Oh oneness separateness identity
      how rare: interrelatedness let it be
       if nothing else a state of mind
         and even that
          so rare.

ROBBER

Companion I've robbed
of everything good in life
 not everything good
  there *are* layers of good
   but it seems that way
    that I am the thief
     as my work habits spread life out to
      an impossibility
       and everything becomes myself
        when I've robbed you of the hours needed
         to fulfill yourself
          the dream of art explored
           becomes reality.
            Forgive me if ever you can
           but for such loss can
          "the spirit of forgiveness"
         ever enter?
        I can only continue on the course I'm on
       take charge of the chaos of
      my life in art, my confession
     do the best I can to at least succeed somewhat with that.
    That I can leave you as something that did work
   the sounds in songs in words
  will never be a substitute
 for the blood of life.
It comes down to
  I wish I could give back to you.
    The least I can do is be one with you
       instead of two.

DRAMA OF THE HEART

When is a heart a drama?
When it stops beating?
When it is caressed?
When it is sacrificed?
When it is doing its thing now?

A PERSPECTIVE

Divinely inspired means
a lot of divinity:
too much sugar.
Inspired means
a lot of humility
with lots of help from
an unknown source.
Isn't it odd
that someone should have the gall
to call it God.
I prefer gratitude
for a pleasant surprise.
When at last
I'm not pushing anything
too much.
Just part of
what's going on.

↝

It's fun and
PULSOPOSITIVE!

BATS

My mind is a bat cage.
They're all in there trying to get out.
How can I free anything.
How can I wait till dawn?
Deep breathing in
      and
out.

My mind is a bat cave
they're all in there sleeping
I go back to bed in my head.

GLAD

We stared at the large photo on the wall
of the planetarium display
at all those tilted specks of galaxies.
That's *all of them put together*
my son said.
No, the label said, this is just *one teeny* area
somewhere in the vicinity of the Big Dipper,
Ursa Major. Big Bear indeed.
All those galaxies and we're out towards
the edge of just one. What to make of it.
My ego has been cut down to size.
Some humility creeps in.
In fact if I could really see it maybe my ego
doesn't really exist. Right now
I don't know what it is.

SEEING DRINK

There's nowhere out
but in
and in there I find
an infinite being.
The imagination of mind
and the totality of body –
seeing
there is beyond me
a Sacred Sea –
mists, clouds, the rise of water
storms, rain, flow
water pure coming down
and then up in the springs
to drink.
As I drink now.

HANDS

Time, lucent traveler,
hand of my hands
loving hands, strong
clean, but not meticulously so,
a couple rings on fingers
which he takes off
loving so.

Grasp the fondle of things
the handle, the dangle, danger
check the temperature
warmth is best.
When you feel, when you feel it,
when you feel it up.

CONNECTED

The pulling of covers off the tomb of God
revealed a scratchy surface.
Only the known world was there
so I didn't feel insignificant in that
everything was related.
How his death enlightened me
dead to be reborn to interrelatedness
to the stars, so many stars
scattered out ad infinitum.
That was the mystery of the surface of this tomb
this bit of hard scratchy earth
concrete, flat rock, surface
of everything under. Everything dependent
and swinging in cycles. I covered what I had uncovered.
Again.

RIGHT NOW ALIEN

It is possible to transform encounters with Spacecraft.
Same old boring space junk out there.
Don't you get tired of throwing alien parts out the window?
And their monotonous 40's and 50's smart deco
    furnishings which crowd their little warped vehicles.
Somehow they never got modern but remained just
    a step ahead of their dated Hollywood serials.
Their entire alien world never got beyond a B movie.
There's so much of their stuff in the antique stores
    the prices are falling.
Oh for a true contemporary presence of the far-out
    of their advanced handiwork and incredibly fertile minds.
But you don't see any of it, because it doesn't exist here.
It is always backwards from our imagination.
If anything is going to change it, modernize it,
    bring it up to date, even make it all contemporary.
We will, you and I, let's work on it right now.
Put our thoughts together and come up with a twist
    in their history. It's about time.
Finally, a fresh true real-time view of outer-space life
    as it *is*.

G.O.D.

It was a rare following that clocked God's positives.
Most of them put him down or crucified his D.
His O was left in the middle, vibrant as always
humming, connecting everything around.
But the G, they could concentrate on that –
the green, the gardening the guh-guh-guh-guh
the good. Yes, all of these things made everything up,
the guh-guh-guh-guh, the Oh, the Oh-h-h-h
and the D, the Damn D. The Doom, the Death.
    They concentrated on the first two, but realized it was all
    one word.

TO THE END

As the flowers pop in and out
 the flowers pop in
  and men and women pop in
   the world turns over the same color
    but warmer
     and with thousands of do good things
      in their head
       do good things feel good –
        things go to their head
         they think their brains are biggest
          and best – in their heads
           they think their brains are best
            and they're better off than most
             and the best
              they think they're the best
               and what'll they do when each
                religion tells them it's best
                 each religion the best!
                  They reproduce in giant numbers
                   and fight to the sword
                    fight to death by the sword
                     and with God knows any weapon
                      plows and dirt be doomed
                       and that's what we are
                        that's where we are
                         guess what we are
                          that's what we are
                           fighting egos to the end
                            to the end
                             fighting big egos to the end
                              to the end.

JUST FRIENDS

We drifted apart
and became close
in my mind
a residue of reality
stays
remembering someone
adroitly
not just anyone –
a friend.

ON THE WAY

Going endlessly home
to the sky I created
dying to be different
dying.
Loving the risk
 eating the universe
  killing the roaches
   of the sundance marines
    stopping for a fill up
   and then on
  my curious destiny –
a cowboy who's only
visited a ranch
           and yet in his dreams
           everything is real.
               Time to move on
               to where he was going.
               Everything is an excuse
               for everything else.
                   But being honest
                   is my trick,
                  as I pass where I come from
                   on the way to
                   where I'm going.

THE WORD

"The Logos would be made flesh
and dwell among us."
The logos, the log in the log out.
The lug wrench made flesh.
The sound out.
The lugging, the logging, the low gain.
The low goat.
Low ghost.
What is before us is after us.
Paradise in the flow made common.
Come enter me come be me come by me.
Come into my heart, by my heart. Be my heart.
Be my whole heart, skin flesh and bones
alive in the greater knowing I am connected
with the wind blowing.
I want rain and nothing's the same.
Log in. Low gain. Low goes. Lugging. Gusting.
A low gust, breeze pleases.
As I breathe in the very flesh I feel.
That is, I become among us.
Just me being teased by spiritual mentors
by the breeze, knocks me down, unhurt
a low ghost.
A low goes. But not into high.
Seeing simply energy.
Do you see it, the flesh made rotten.
Is now, alive. Flowing life logos.
The word in other words is, the word.
Log in low going goes.
Hey go, breathing in, it enters deeply
goes throughout my body.
Mind clears, the sunlight
bouncing off grape leaves, moves too
with the breeze. Bright light green.
As I enter into it entering me.

᷾

(John 1-14)

RELAX INTO ME

                What grace
            his composure had
        when he was by himself
     and didn't have to worry
  what he looked like
how he acted
where he was
    but could be   just could be   just could be.

GOOD

That *you* are good
and *in* good
and *of* good
is good.
That you are *from* good
and good is from you
that you are within good
vibrate the wisdom of good
and beyond good
bringing everything that is good
to good   is good.

LIMBO DUST

When a person can't pray
everything seems artificial to say.
There is a breeze.
Moving green leaves.
A bird.
A dragonfly.
A plane flying over
distantly.
What is near?
Large ants.
A pepper plant, a dahlia in pots.

GREATER THAN REALITY
in memory of Mario Lanza (1921-1959)

What is your fascination with a supreme being?
It is the union of energy and love
that takes form and everything is dependent on.
Is there a personality in this disclosure?
Yes, in my solitude there is a greater other
who intercedes and directs if I love that sort of thing.

There is a constant coming to life as I live that way.
A movement that is beyond comprehension
taking form in the game of surprise and no surprise.
A speech in the wind, a prompting, a connection
like lifelines of energy, electric knowhow
in the broad expanse of things, a plus, a plus, a minus.
Oscillating, alternating, direct flow,
one with the blood and the electricity of the brain.
Hello Central, an old voice says to me out of the blue
and a song sings its way along.

The imagination will never be stopped
but in a caring fashion, it is greater than reality,
and speaks caves of wisdom in little pieces.

I put together what I can, or see the picture
and don't have to bother, have to be one with it,
released into it which is a determining of myself
in fruitful time, to keep action with it,
be acting with it, however slow moving
as it is always moving into form, into focus
being the prayer of the cat licking itself
the dog lying down to go to sleep
and *an actual voice:*
"Be my love, for no one else will fill this yearning."
(sing to the tune of "Be My Love")

WITH ONE HEART (To Song)

Death of the dead, dead of the dying
Creator of the Wonder Universe
lifting the unliftable by doing the unthinkable,
    exploding the drab
draining the dying, obliterating the abscess of pretense
the weight off my lungs, numbed clarity
    turned into black curtains, raise them, do as
        you do. Power of the waning universe
to pick yourself up and turn me around or,
    stunned by our unthinking lack of gratitude,
don't do anything and let us all come into you,
Buddha ears, unhearing, budding eyes reflecting
the perfect intense yellow non-prickly prickly pear
    cactus flower burst glorious from flat leaves pads,
bees buzzing all into, pollen covered legs,
the light delivery of the intense universe
everything focused now to rid me of my down dejection,
    self-pitying discharge of myself
open to the possible now, that is, can be, is.
Why so sad I can't move? To not move
    is to not kneel down, indent the floor of the cosmos
        with the way sunlight intertwined, the way it is.

It embraces me now realizing at the end of it
I am at the beginning, precious instant, deflowered
    again, given up to the Zeus, the Venus, the older
        Aphrodite, the Isis of memory, the Osiris of the heart
and Jesus, one in all of us whatever it is being, not being,
in peace of love in pieces revealed suddenly breaks whole,
becomes one with the heart, frees, takes off, releases,
comes out, births, as you were, as I am, takes me, free.
I am totally unchanged and free to be who I am –
    compassionate instant. Open doors open all,
willing to be willing to will nothing but open,
be breathing. Everything said is everything said.
Everything said removed forever to breathe
    as I am now in you part of a part of a part
lifted lighted in perfect night. Stars say distance.

I'm left hearing. Conscious. Equal. Giving into.
To get up and work when the night passes as
    everything rises from sleep.
The first breath of appreciation frees.
That is, gives energy. That is truly charged, go.
To love what is obvious, the love around you is me.
My love around you is you, the complete futility of
    being exact. There is only nature, true nature, flowing.
Pain has been removed by not being what it is.
It is alive, what it was that created the uplifting spirit
    as it rings again, sings again sings, sings again.
My heart is a true-love adventure.

TURNING MY BACK

What is depression but a lowering of the spirits
    sky high
when you know there is a world of universes out there
all competing for survival.
I don't wish to survive, I'd rather die
and let them go on battling it out
    over my grave.
They will anyway, rushing with all their energy
    to dominate.
Dominate yourself to oblivion.
Fight it out to the last cause.
Populate yourselves till the universe
is packed with universes and there's no room to budge.
I give it all over to you, what little I can –
    you competitors are the winners.
I'm for peace, unheard of, non-resistance
turning my back on you and your noise
and crying into nature, what's left of it.

MY PIECE OF FLYING SAUCER

What's really important is that the eye be open to the ear
 and the ear be open to the heart.
  The heart whatever it is, be open to the breath.
  The breath be open to the art of the mind.
  The direction of creativity taking over.
  In that the given direction be given.
  Oh heart-intellect, intuition
  it falls from the sky into your lap and you can get up,
 let it fall to the floor and be swept away,
or recognize, oh mind of the art, this seed,
 Unusual Object fell from the sky
  or earth essence made manifest.
   Mother Sky, Father Earth, Moon Goddess why?

    Practice allows me to recognize
   when something different approaches.
  As everyone may, learn to
 appreciate extraterrestrial originality.
There is no known marking on this thing in my lap,
 this piece of equipment. Of what use is it?
  How big is it? What material is it made of?
   Where, Creator, did it come from?
    Can I trust it?
     What shall I do with it?
    I look at it. Oh, I hear something it says.
   A heart beating inside. How exciting!
  This is the most interesting thing that's ever happened to me.
  My God, it's breathing.
Such long slow breaths.
 What lights! What markings!
  Oh, it says for me to . . follow my art,
   my art of mind.
    The direction of creativity taking over.
     The giving of it, take up
    and build on it, you, me. Yes,
   We.
  Here it is, I hope you find it as curious as I did.
  I just took it and went from there
 where it and I followed, fostering.
  This is how I got here.

I am truly appreciative.
 Life has a lot of joy when something new
  arrives on the scene.
   It happens almost every other day
  to me.
 Here.
 What do you think?
 Or is it just
fun?

SIMPLICITY

Don't come apart –
be one.
One wonderful
one.
One to be the child I am
one to be the leader of the child
one to be the adult
one to be the leader of the adult
one to be one
with everything I am
one to be the adult
I am
one to be circumscribed
one to be the stars
one to be the planets on the elliptic
one to be one
with the love
the love full of love
unashamed
no harm ever meant in love
 no harm energies in love
  only love
  one
   given in love
    don't come apart
     given in part
      to power

power in love
of the one
wonderful
one.
Given in love
cannot come apart
one
in
love.
One
wonderful
word.
Power
in
love.
One
wonderful
love.
One
in
one.
One
 wonderful
 one.
  One
  in
    love.

EPITHALAMIUM: BLESSED, TRULY KISSED
for Ariel and Christopher   July 20, 2002

    That two might be one
    is charming fun.
    At one to be one with the world.
   At two to be two too.
   At three all things are blessed
    and the ancient architecture
   is solid on the ground.
   The round, dirt, earth
   learn from first.
  As you come up from the ground
  and tower into a church
 if everything is moving and you're breathing
 you must be alive.
 What a surprise, both of you alive
 both of us alive.
Alive to meet with the air and go somewhere.
 Where shall we go
how about to the church
and let's get married
you and I what a time to be a surprise in.

Shall we invite all our friends and family too.
You mean all our family of friends
and shall we all get married and become one family.
Let us all accept the vows of love and
   compassion for each other, wow what a vow!
Hello and the Earth and Air are married too
and the Sun and Stars, Night and Day
any way and every way, directions and one way –
one way blessed by the sheer being alive
alive dance and well. Who isn't married, tell all
one is married to two, I mean one and one is two
and we're all thrown in in a happy marriage of
  first things first.
A man, a boy, and a woman, a girl.
Well it sounds to me like the Garden of Eden
which is what it always will be, paradise.
Yes, right here on Earth there is a true path to follow
full of growing things and surprise.

May you love, blessed, leap life dance congrat-
 ulations, felicitations, celebrations.
May you love life blessed in the now, the eternal
 now made more precious by your presence,
everything with flowers and bouquets and gifts galore
and dancing on a vibrant floor, and receptions and
renewing of faiths and good health and kisses of love,
embraces and passion for knowing the knot is tied
the rings blessed, the first step into the present taken
 cakes cookies feasts and seasons –
July a joy when the sun and blue sky and clouds
 and breezes and misty rain and caresses and
 steps through the arch of tomorrow and today is
 everyday discovering
 one love two love love above in this present
 special living present, love that
 two might be one
 is charming fun,
 oh lovely present be
 in the lovely delicious present.
 By power of the Creator Universe
 love loves freely blessed
 truly kissed.

 ༒

JULY TWENTY SECOND

 July, jewel of this month blushed tomato.
 Already time to reap the garden, as if we
 haven't been picking from it earlier, as it
 changes, working after work in its Earth presence
 the borders of sky lifting the spirits high
 clouds drawing rain out, spectacular sunset.
 Everybody's time is all time. Everybody's time
 is all time.

FEMININE ENDING

America with your rituals of indifference
as greed incorporates your flower
    what happened to your dream of technology?
        Your hope that every birthday gets a cake?
Children with no food.
Retirees with no pot to piss in.
Everybody working at Macdonald's
and hamburgers giving people heart attacks
living too long on less life
as the water makes you free
your burning tongue
    the Stature of Liberty on fire?
Too many people have stunted the Earth
and the animals need protection as they
    run for cover
as people buy every product they can get
    from China –
Lao Tzu said "When knowledge and cleverness appeared
great hypocrisy followed in its wake."

The ship of many   cuts through the waters
    and kills the fish
and everyone gets out on the populated shore
refugees on their own planet.
Give me some hope: everything is spiritual
if Nature commands
and we all share and share alike
when disaster comes.
Ego breaks down on the corner when asking for food.

What happened to your mother, America,
"Centre of equal daughters, equal sons" –
the Whitman of the hour?
What happened to the body of your land?
Build a better listening device, the ear
hear with what you see
take the minute and slow down. →

Quietly. Breathe to make the air
    pure and the water clear,
limit your numbers to what we can replenish
joyfully, responsibly,
"Perennial with the Earth"
    carefully
        prayerfully.

TOUGH TURKEY
(In memory of Dessie Goodell,
        Grandma born July 25, 1889)

Tom Turkey totaled. Or maybe he wasn't Tom.
Dick Turkey done in.
Too old to be good.
Now roasted.
Maybe I'll make turkey soup tomorrow
    lots of it.
A 22 pound turkey a year and a half old.
After gutting, 15 pounds.
I'm telling you, guts make up a lot of us.
Joel cut the head off as I held old Tom.
Axe sharpened.
My little folding Gerber knife sharpened.
Water boiling in the big galvanized tub.
Dipped him in heavy as he was, he floated.
Took out feathers, for hours.
I have my procrastination to thank for this
tough turkey.
Putting it off getting someone to help me.
Well when I'm dying and I haven't gotten
    around to that big task
it'll be too late.
Maybe I'll join the turkey in the sky, or in
some deep canyon
where his repeated gobble
and my self-pitying sighs will amuse
the coyotes – and fall on deaf ears
of the dry river bed.

ROOT LEVEL

I announce a Dodo who will become president of
    the billionaire dodos
and the Do Nothings will bask in their paradise of silk
    and rub jewels against their flesh as they
    scratch each other's buttocks.
I announce jackasses heehawing *"I'm the Lord"*
    and raking in billions from their lawn of deceit.
I announce the king of announcers spreading hate
    like oil over the land of our fathers
I announce the mothers of our time refusing
    to be mothers and fathers abandoning their kids
to the sickness of poverty.
I announce the obvious as the obvious announces itself
    as 10,000 tons of cocaine are confiscated at the borders
and 100 thousand tons of it are elsewhere ingested.
    I announce ego and greed ruling the world as everyone
has said so many do, so few are left
    to accomplish so much
overwhelmed by the need of commonsense, I announce
my lack of confidence in myself to do anything at all
but get down on my knees and have my knees
get down on their knees to announce to the ants,
    What can we do?
I announce the question what little can I do
turning over the field of my mind, planting a white pine tree
    that was our Christmas tree
turning over in my mind, the berries that survived
must be planted, the little blue spruces transplanted
for our son to plant, if they survive and grow
    on his land.
The air announces a breeze across my back as I sit
    and announce nothing.
The crickets announce their repeated chirps as I have
    nothing to say.
The dog in the distance in the middle of this night
    barks and my dog at my feet growls
while I say, you know, I'm not really a pessimist
    it just doesn't show
that someday somehow if I keep a really open mind

I may have something to announce, something I have been given
    to announce
from the corn out there almost ready to pick
the tomatoes and bell peppers and jalapeños, green beans
cucumbers and carrots. Perhaps the carrots have the answer
growing in the ground.
A sound, an announcement
    yet to make.

A PASTORAL

Good spirit has returned to the chapel on the hill in my left brain
    a quiet breeze, interlude, slightly overcast sky.
The organ fills my ears, is it a marriage or celebration of Easter?
    Surprises by laughter from the service
        floating down the river to my right brain
        and all coalesces throwing out meaning
    real as real as tea, a bit of sugar or honey, and milk.
    A pastoral connects my two brains into one.
    There is no chapel, god is the reality
        running through my veins
    the pulsing throughout my body life
the breeze, the door of nature opening ever opening
    to free me to see, the warmth that is
love ever in the bell I ring and the violin orchestra
    and dog barking to be let back in
back in to my dreams, my dreams of everything connected
    everything awake.

THE ROUND ROBIN OF LOVE

Cocks are all over in the round robin of loving
and so are hairy pussies.
Oh the flower of aching love, ache
until a bee comes along to gloriously invade
and everyone in the sex network is excited
and there's much buzzing around in the gossip of pleasure.

FOR THE COWBOY BUDDHA ON HIS 67(TH) BIRTHDAY
for Gino Sky, birthday August 6

The fence is always straddley-er on the greener side.
   Here is what we do:
 we'll be dead in the Onion City of Paradise.
Paradise: when the two rivers meet in a confusion of species.
  Species: all species all species all species.
    The river runs upward and downward
and joins in the two cites of Monach-ma and Monach-ma Glory.
  Singing up flowing to a shattering waterfall.
Birds winging in doubt, owls sitting there
    the Queen and King arguing over their debt.
        Rivers flowing up and down.
  Trees what species, cycads gonads palm trees.
 What color are the men and women, what color are the little
    boys. The little girls.
 At this point there were not too many men and women.
     There were not too many people.
Purple dawn. Electrified. Misted
     a perfect rainbow to the West.
 Double rainbow, gifted, high
from mountain side to lowering valley.
   Rare, on this your birthday. On my friend's birthday
  in this mountainside of paradise.
    We are not arguing. We've never had a cross word.
     Creativity spills through our lives like rivers.
Rivers going up and down, friendship, rising
  to a crashing waterfall:
 it is surprising what life lets live.
     That it should come to your 67(th) birthday
and I'm 67 too. That we pull through
in our separate paradise. Oh where there are onions
   and corn to pick, and all the best vegetable
"veggie tables." Mini farm, large heart.
    Friendship in the dawn, friendship in the heart
closer than brothers, than sisters even in the
flowing river up the rushing river down
   the waterfall, the desire, the flowing out.
      The space that doesn't exist between us.
 Don't take light of it, but make light of it
deep underground stream artesian awake.

As your novels and stories write themselves out Cowboy Buddha
                  and poems and songs celebrate –
as my poems open like fans shake hands like friends
      build to their raga ending when the duende release
leaves you on higher ground than you stood before –
           thanks to higher ground that cloudy mountain side
   that obscure dream turns into rain
                          the mist with sun in early early morning
     turns into the rainbow that is from me to you.
Thanks to inordinate power, the creative spirit
          of the heart, of the wings of the remembering mind
   of the paradise of two and all friends, all where
true honest dreams are fulfilling, fulfilling.
    Crashing down waterfall from the two rivers of our dreams.
        Reached the same age, together, apart in our high spirits
                body dreams, appreciative. Great great
      gratitude on both sides of the dawn.

MAKING UP PLACES

You've gotta be in cahoots with the place names
in order to spit them out,
like Crack of Dawn, Kansas
Elysium Fields, Norway and Sin Sin, Vermont.
Have you ever been to I Can Dwarf You, Nebraska?
Or Cow Cow Boogie, California?
Where do you hail from: I hail from
My Mother's Womb, Iowa
where Frostbite Canyon feeds in to
the Abercrombie Draw.
I'm Tired of Making Up Names, Texas,
which is where I was originally from
before Ralph Edwards came along and called it
Truth or Consequences, New Mexico.

WISHFUL STINKING

He is forever pulling negatives out a positive stump. The stump thought the skunk stunk when the skunk didn't let a stink. There was no stink and yet he found a skunk and made it stink. He insisted the stump stunk too when there was no stink at all. He went around sticking stink on things and accusing the skunk who didn't stink of producing the stink he thought was there. The stump was as confused as the skunk and the stink that wasn't a stink was nowhere but in his stinking thinking. In reality the skunk was very positive about the whole thing and was actually quite beautiful. And the stump was just a stump full of history. And there was no stink at all. Except in his head he carried around heavy as lead. Stinking, stinking thinking. Thinking stinking when there was no stink. Thinking stinking thinking when there was no stink. Thinking stinking thinking when there was only something truly beautiful, truly beautiful.

WAR AND PEACE

The following will kill anything:
    Eriptoid Patoxy

The following will allow all
to love each other and refuse weapons:
    Bali-hall i-halli-ho C Major.

DIE OH LOG

Please help me and give me strength –
I don't know what to do without you.
I'll do what I always do, do without you.

SOME CALL IT GRACE

    One who, as only you love me, loves me
  with no heat of false heart, no weapon
   but with the warmth of understanding wrongs fail
 in the long run, which is every hour of lived life.
Open my arms to it, wide in bed, looking up in the darkness
after coyotes' high yippin' wakes me
 sweeping the air with my arms, no false heart
  just the science of acceptance for now.
   The art of accepting the gifts as nature surrounds,
    I fade into it and work through the anguish
     that I can't get the big thing done –
      small steps guide me if I take them.
       Why fight what helps some one else?
       And keeps me open to one, open to love.

ASS FIRST THROUGH THE COSMOS

Be the message you are.
Hitch your butt to a star.

JUST FOR FUN

    My God is square, with a big nose.
    What is yours?
    A carrot up his butt for ornament
    and a permanent hard-on.
    He plays with his sexuality
    and whoops! He winks.
    I feel mighty uncomfortable
    talking about God.

UNDER STARS

What is the power that bends and sees
  that fleshes things out
   that fills out the universe with intermingling cells
   that holds on in stellar winds and *is* stellar winds
  horizontal lightning, heavenly blue morning glory
 in the spirit of interconnectedness, the rain
  the rain that falls, the water that trickles down
 in the mountain, the power greater than ourselves
 our human cells that our egos say were in command of
but the electricity in our bodies is the same
 as all that wrapped through the universe which
  in greater energies calls, causes us to sweat
   causes me to humble down, bow down my efforts
    to be of concerning grace, to get one with the spirits
     of the ancient Tao, the buzzing in the Buddha's ear,
      the Muse at the poet's command, commanding the poet
     as she addresses her love, her love affair
      her passion, her musicianship, the dance
       of the music in her ear. Her ear to his, his
        to hers, hearing Apollo's heart, Walt leaping continents
         in only the mind as the electricity of imagination
         bends and warps, tells stories, frees
        and the Muse, *musica,* lips in the ear dancing,
         is of presence, I ask, face on floor, for help,
         in the immediate universe of the stars,
         help from the Universe, as I get up, into it.
       Society is help and nothing else, as going it alone
      falls down, kills and self-kills. I ask, humbly
     to be connected, reconnected, hand over head, leading
    direction in my power to be good. Every step of the way
   on this planet, this little part of a larger part,
    heart beats with it, in the countenance of love
     suddenly breaks down, everything breaks down
      melts in the eyes, as is pleasure. Science
       musicianship, the art of listening
        which is a command, commands now
         keep yourself in healthy example, genuinely
          without pushing anything, unless you're helping someone
           move into their new house
            and then you're lifting, really lifting.

  It does snake through various presences,
   cells willing to communicate, if only I could see them
  ever such
  distances: what do I know about anything
 as peculiar and compelling as that.
 But call on it, it commands me
 in all honesty, to stand up and do it.
This work around the house, around the property
inside my head and out. Efficiency
 flows in like water, carrying electricity with it.
  Somewhere all these stars from a wand
  the merry magic princess waves and
  I follow, disappear
   and the real stars hang out at night.
   Overhead I see them, waving to me, now,
   or rather, pinpointing their mysteries
   now, now, now.

        ɔ

    Who cares what shoes you wore
    in 1982?

        ɔ

COLORATURA BOSSA NOVA

What is my place in the universe?
Hanging on to the tara, the tora, the toura?
Coloratura bossa nova
  bass or blues?
Low or low blow, high or a balloon.

A BIG MEETING

Where are they meeting, why?
The Gods have appointed me their Fool.
I am flattered, but the pay is lousy.
The Gods are meeting in the sky
or where are they meeting, why.

They don't tell me everything
sometimes they don't tell me anything.
I surmise something is going on.
Still I'm expected to work full-time
everything geared to what they tell me
if they tell me anything, with that I'm to be satisfied
despite the pay.
There's a rumbling going around
there's a shake-up going down
but it's not people getting arrested
it's more than that: the animals of the Earth
and the plants are involved, I mean
all the plants, all the animals
it seems it's our entire biosphere.
What are they saying, what are they doing
what am I certain of?
They're sitting in a circle, somewhere there
that I know. They're all involved,
not just one, not even just two or three
all of them, and of course, wherever they are
they're facing each other and it's animated
what are they saying, but they're speaking
and everyone else listening, one at a time.
Intent, they're all involved.
What was that rumbling?
Something close.

The Gods are all meeting
where are they meeting, why?
They're in a circle. Destiny is involved.
All living things. Vibrations, a ringing
bell. What am I supposed to do,
when will they tell me.
What am I supposed to do in this job.

It is a job, they tell me that
which ever one of them speaks, or all together.
They tell me to stick to it, Fool.
Fool, like Shakespeare, no not that smart.
Just do these silly things, maintain a sense
    of humor, a living sense of humor at
all times, but it amounts to when I can.

And I'm supposed to write about it no matter what.
And I do. What are they saying, perhaps
if I go out now, ring my own bell
breathe deeply, relax, and observe,
keep myself alert, and open
it will come, it will come to me
some sense of what they are doing
what is going on, the Pleiades above
faintly, a group, a cluster, a meeting
what are they doing, they're talking, it's
downright animated, 12 of them I guess because
I can't see clearly, up the slope of the Sandias
I can't be funny about this. But it's my job
the pay is lousy, as I repeatedly say
    but it is an honor:
the Gods are meeting in the sky
or where are they meeting, why
    here on Earth, right here, I hear it
I'll tell you more when I hear it.
Careful, one of them is speaking.
Yes they're listening, they're listening
all nature is involved, this Earth,
their very own planet they have connections with
the Universe with the massive other meeting
of other Gods, maybe they're all meeting, everyplace
actually they're having a good time, you know Gods.
This meeting, Earth's, and those others, other places
    far out, they're meeting too.
They're having a good time, but there's something
serious going on. I hear them. I hear them, kind of.
Wow it's close. I'll tell you more when I know it
that's my job, and it scares me sometimes. →

But I have to stay alert, sober and open to it,
to every word. Just like every other fool in the universe.
We can tell each other if and when we find out.
We can have our own meeting. Right now.
I'm certainly not the only fool around.
Let's get together. What was that?
Why are they laughing when things are so serious.

If they're meeting, let's meet. I'll see you soon.
You tell me what you think is going on: I'm all ears.
The Gods are meeting right now.

MY EGO

My ego tells me to not work
to fuck around in the dirt
to come clean with nothing
and rest on my ass.

My ego tells me to dream
about past displeasures
and not wrestle with anything
especially now.

My ego tells me to pick up a drink
to make doing nothing more than it is
everything's at a standstill and there's
nothing but dreaming about the future.

There's nothing present when
my ego takes over,
only the loss of every minute,
the vacuum of now
when I'm trying to guide
a sinking boat or rather
just miserably
going down with it.

GIFT GIVING

     Oh lovely light of the world, world of lovely light
    enter my spirit and fight with the darkness –
   it will take some struggle, but what do I know.
   You may rinse everything out with light
  and renew the spirit. You may just be
 and exalt the burning sunset
lifting up and exchanging the dark for light
the deep depression pit home destroyed
as Shiva danced it out, as a Kachina of the Sun
came and went and left the children happy,
 the young parents at home with each other,
  the fires burning in the sunset relinquishing
   to the darkness and stars, at least the stars again.
    "I give you the stars, you unhappy wretch.
     I give you the light that was and will be again
      and again and again and again, I give you the stars."

☙

STAMPEDE OF MORONS

Gates of a high-rise century
open freely, open freely
let century out
as cartoon energies hit the dirt.
All comes crashing down in the now.
I will seriously deal with
a groaning planet.
Too many of us vying for existence
elbowing each other to death.
It is a stampede
of morons.
Even the brightest
are dull witted.
What a shame
what a crying shame.
Such wonder gone to dust.

EATING THE LIGHT

I solidified my union with the darkness
by eating the light.
There's nothing wrong with darkness
in the shadow, in the shadow.
I lie here dreaming of the light, digesting, digesting.

MEDITATIONS THAT DON'T MEAN ANYTHING

My head is eaten up by my heart
and that's the way it has been.
The winner.

Love comes out of nowhere
where the heart is.

Why must my mind reject feelings
pushing them down where
my heart is.

What is my heart
other than a pump?

My head is strong
my heart is heavy
my body is weak.

In the middle of the night
what am I doing when I should be
sleeping?

COMING OUT OF IT

Is everything funny, she asked, refusing to laugh.

No, he said, tragedy sustaining his family for years.
The sky rose up in a scatter of blue tears.
Were they tears of laughter   or pain?
No, they were just tears.
Then he cracked a smile but it was only after
    stewing in a pit for a long long while.
And she refused to laugh, and suppressed a giggle
    so hard she almost exploded.
Then she saw the lousy side of things
    and had no urge to laugh at all.
And he laughed until the tears ran down his cheeks
and floated up to London where things were always funny
and then into space where the sun formed
    rainbows in the misty evening –
the dissipation of tears!
Natural beauty took precedent over all their fears.

At last some smile will come
whether you put it there or it just pops up from somewhere.
But what curves we are thrown!
Life is a curved ball, she said, as he caught her.
We might as well make the best of it
    up in the sky looking down. Why the frown?
Nature doesn't laugh. Well, my dog smiles.
Who is to say what the mood of that cactus is.
The plants are always happy after a rain.
Let's ease off into nowhere when we go:
she laughed and he didn't –
there's something awfully funny about that.
There were little giggles, a lot that day
    in all the play at work.
That's something he learned from not being drunk
    all the time.

In fact, she saw life exactly for what it was, what a buzz.
Life is a gas, if you just don't think about it, he thought.
She smiled when he didn't say anything.
At last there was laughter in his eyes.

HUMMINGBIRDS AND TRUMPET VINES

I demand presence, physical presence.
I demand a non-god god
a different god, one that appears first for me
    and stays around.
Oh dear, do I have to feed it?
Does it have to look like a human being
    but glowing somehow?
Hell, what about Nature.
God oozes out of Nature.
Something keeps me company
and comforts me when I go out
    and sit on the portal –
and the fruit trees and morning glories and
    humming birds and trumpet vines
are all there.
Something is so big and wonderful, you know
it doesn't need me,
though I've done some manicuring
    here and there.
Where is this God.
In the seeking I find.
If only I could accept the truth coming through.
The avenue of escape into reality.
The now one wonderful
    of this occasion.
The door which is always open
and is therefore not a door
a doorway which is not even that –
an openness.

CARTOON

He was crazy as a loon
a baboon
a dog wearing pantaloons –
it was all Loony Tunes.

PARTNERS RETURN

Great Haunted Trails of the Northern mesquite
guide me back where I want to be
on the path of the new to me, but old to my partners
who know what they're talking about
and are full of history –
stories that illuminate the present with the past.

Before it's too late, it's too late.

Great haunted trails of my imagination
are sparked by real experience of old
and some younger but they've been there, done that
in the country heavy with hunting experience
and the trailways of the bold, the scared, the persistent.

Before it's too late, it's too late.

Where are you, someone who has something to say
who is not just today full of the trivia of work
that leads to shopping, life that is purchased things?
Or is there never a return to the living past in the present
a continuity of place in the ghosts and resting states
of the pioneer entire families and lessons learned
from farming land traveling, scary borders of the mind
where the stars stretch down their nightly panoply
and plead with the spirit, let us have place.
Love the voices of the past and let us hear each
for once, partners on this journey, here we are at last.

Before it's too late, it's too late, let it be.

⁓

MOON HAIKU

Mooning the moon with
my moon haiku –
ass first, pale white.

WHOLE

Holier than Thou I was until
the Thou became holier than me.

So I analyzed holy: sacred, hallowed, whole:
the whole damned thing. Undamned. Thingless.

Everything is whole. Just whole.
Part of it up down sideways and forward.

What is my focus. My focus is you
because you're holier than me:
you are the whole, including me.

So out there where you are,
I can let you draw me to you in
unending embrace which is the love of all
entwined. The lover's secret is wholeness.

༄

ENLIGHTENMENT IS THE PATOOTIE

Enlightenment is the patootie
when the bathroom odor of yesterday
has dissipated into the desert air of today.
And you can see like a thorn in the side of an eyeball
does not see anything but just is.
As I observe everything around me observing me
without caring two figs for my existence.
And I fade into what I'm doing
as long as I'm doing something
and stick to it which is not my usual way
of doing things, I suddenly
am doing something and do it all the way through
much to my surprise
much to the evidence in my eyes, that I'm not dreaming.
I'm awake.

NOW A MUSE

      Muse, God of my Gods, amused, who are you?
     Moo-cow muse, antelope muse,
    woodpecker on the telephone pole muse
     cottonwood tree tops, table cloth of embroidered fruit
    covered up fresh growth of cut down cherry shrubs
   upturned outdoor pool-form muse
  vein of my vein inside of my inside
every detail of my life remembered, unremembered –
muse-stream flow of eternal jazz making up
     the universe from a prior lead song, the music in it
catches with the wind, the wind muse, the power
    that leaves me and never comes back, breaks its
        negative force, and returns muse, once and for all
with not so much serenity as discovery, what
    is just around the corner, what is just,
the right muse, bends me away into:
 Muse is use. Use the power that comes to you, use it well.
  Tell what it tells. And how it's so.
   It will tell itself, the tale of the muse.
    The funny thing that happened on the way
       to where I'm going.

A BODY DISCOVERED

    The karma dusters have organized themselves around
           the pitfalls of eternity.
    Oh fall into the fall into the fall into the fall.
The wheel of a thousand wheels wheels out of existence.
     You are too abstract. Nail this thing down.
           Who shot who?
    Nobody shot anybody, but a body was found.
         Was it a dead body.
         A body was found.
           Who was it?
     It was the corpse of the Universe.

IMAGE NATION

The power of the imagination:
it hoists vowels.
It staccatos consonants
and slings misery out of joy.
Builds castles out of stone
    or did I say soap.
Wash your brain with it.
Get back to the soul, female
given to me by the Lord above
and the Lord below
and the Lord In-Between.
I'm closer to the Lord In-Between
that curious sexless object of power
that is all sex.
After sex mostly rather than before.
That is the driving itch from below.
The below lord, just as relevant.
Kid me not, they are all one
as names disappear in the landscape of beauty.

Oh, the Emerson tie in to place and magic
where America can never return again.
After sex is most of my day
most of my week.
Right now in fact: it's a long
dry period
but the desert exists to teach us
sustenance.
How else can you appreciate something
    unless you're hungry?
The Lord above and the Lord In-Between
permeate the fabric of the universe
built upon the lord below
which disappears with gravity,
whirling Earth.
Words disappear in the universe.
How restricted to Earth or Earths.
How curious, characteristic of us humans.

The cat, no, the dog, not really
the plants whisper.
If there is no love, there is no you.
What can I do to help alleviate this guilt?
 "I forgive you," all three lords combine to say.
 The power of the imagination
    shall dominate the Earth
 and save it from its human self.

A GENTLEMAN BEGGAR

I wish I could believe
but I can't:
I go through the motions
and oceans roll over
but there is no cause and effect.
Things just happen
along with themselves.
But I cannot deny
the role of the universe
in it.
I cannot deny
my insignificance in the scale of things
and in that is
some hope
and let it go
in power and love intertwined.
May it carry me along with it
gently.

HUM JOY

happiness is a thrill taken seriously
over a longer period of time

FALL MORNING GLORY

               Flower of the Universe
              blooming through everything
            with your energy of delight,
            dancing in the morning like
          a heavenly blue morning glory on
             the scraggly vine, now
          in the fall, all colors, all beauties
         as I understand you
        only in looking at you,
        heavenly blue now ridged with rose
       as you suddenly become
everything but this flower –
in your dance in the mind in the energy of love
  as your dance in the energy of love
        loves my looking at you
           otherwise we know I'll never know
         you as a gift, the growing
          dancing in the wind gift
          outpouring of love
            into my emptiness, flowing
           blooming, turning me into
          this evanescent flower
          as I am in love in you
          with you. As it is every
          giving minute of the day
          grace of wit, gift, living
          flower of the universe
          a dance together.

REALITY NOTE

Bug-infested heaven
wasn't what I thought it'd be
but it was organic
as hell.

LUBRIDERM

I used to like Lubriderm
until I found a fish in it
dead from the Creation
proof of God.

That's what I needed
proof
so now as I sit here
hands stinking
I should be happy
instead of wishing
I'd bought unscented.

SCREW LOOSE LOGIC

Where did the mind jump to
when it got away?
And what center of mine
is deteriorating now?
I'm fortunate
to be alive
I mean if you like life.
What do you mean "like"?
There isn't any liking
there's just a great big hug.
I mean an intense huge hug
constantly.
Don't you think
you're carrying things
a bit too far?
I mean farther than farther
than far? Whoops
I swallowed the whole thing
down.
Wasn't that the purpose
of drinking when you're thirsty?
Isn't that the purpose
of the celibate life?
I have withdrawn from
the debating society.
It was called
"Screw you logic."
Now I'm just a member
of a dance group that doesn't
dance any more.
We just get together
and talk about old times.
No, I caught myself lying
which is not unusual.
The society I belong to
is anonymous.
Poets Anonymous –
there you go.
I finally
I mean finally,
which is right now,
get the truth out.

WHAT IS IT

What is it
surrounding you
ever expanding
subtracting,
a mathematician of
a higher order.

How do we do the dance then
that we do:
do we dance?
I'm telling you the truth –
I dance
I say weird things
make up languages or rather
sounds.

The dog gets excited
and accompanies me in this –
we create myths.
Can someone who is not on
this path of love
to love
understand me?
I don't know
But I elucidate
what I'm on
by telling the path,
take me.
As long as I do
the walking
and less of
the talking.

ROSWELL NORTH

One Horse Road
Salt Creek Road
Raton
Los Alamos
Eden Valley
Red Bluff Road
Cottonwood Road
Star Grass Road
Dona Ana
slow hill into
hill into
hill into
Vaughan, New Mexico
half-way home.

EONS SPEAK

The flower of having passed "through Paradise in a dream . . . and if he found that flower in his hand when he awoke . . . and what then?"
– Samuel Taylor Coleridge

>Flowers passing through eternity, eons beckon,
>time calling to itself "Energy obliterates us, neighbor."
>The flower of insistence blooms and soon is gone,
>every phase of itself, it is seed and bud, flower and seed.
>Light propels things, as the unseeing universe speaks.
>I am where I am in developing, as energy is all
>and eyes on planets form to see me. Eyes
>have opened up the planting of time, in seasons.
>Back to Earth and similar residences. The miracle
>persists. It isn't perfect but it allows flowers to form.
>And grazing animals. The cow. The sheep. The raven.
>The squirrel. All eat. All animals & planets. Isn't this human
>>a character? His ego will kill him. Flowers of light
>>passing through eternity. Eons speak.

☙

LOVE EVOLVE

>Allah
>all of
>olive
>all of us
>malagueña
>oligarchy of gods
>Gods in the Gardens of Spain
>in the Gardens of my home, Mother's,
>Garden of Garden of Lenore's
>as all things come up from the Earth
>to kiss the Sun.

IN THE STARS

Deepest inquiry into the rock that feeds as minds in outerspace connect. Oh say I know you, I've seen you before carrying out the groceries at the local store.

You became my divine inspiration as archaic wisdom spread through the universe. Can I have some? We modernized ourselves by keeping trim, we the twins of old transformed into brothers that is pretend brothers, rather we became friends.

Out of nowhere how high the moon dancing in the dark. Exactly like you hey there it had to be you all of me I'm confessin' on the sunny side of the street fools rush in all the things you are whispering speak low but not for me.

Guide best man, best friend two stars hang out and carry on the research, is there a black hole between them?

No it would suck us into it but something keeps us apart, just daily reality of living, taking our space on planet Earth. Wait there's something over my shoulder singing these old songs, keeping my memory alive with blood the food the excitation of nerve endings, the meaning of life it is our father coming from our mother standing in a universal energy way over me with arms of the galaxies around our shoulders, we live in each other's presence without being there. Such is the power of the loving imagination.

Someone greater than I by the dawn said "I love you and that is all I have to do" and I said I want to and I do, as if we friends are a wedding, a best wedding a sacred ceremony of the present from the rock that eats everything, the volcanic tragedy evil self-centered minds do evil self centered things as all hope forgives and the turn of love surprises, rips dawn out and replaces it with the morning stars fading into the sun, two of us in mutual partnership from separate sides of the river, you hunt elk or is it wisdom, I dig a hole trying to find the septic tank. Someone has to do the romantic discovery the oldest activity of all. We are better than I. We can do things better though apart. As long as coming together takes form over the phone, over any way we can condition it

Long live our future now as now is everything it ought to be because it wants to be what it is, a celebration of our togetherness in our separateness. As we discover, accepting love is easy as saying it. This is what I want to do, love fills my cup even when things are the most empty. My marriage forever, my friendship in the stars that wrap around my shoulders keeping me warm at night. Rock of the universe whirling through space, rock of ages bless be the tie that binds, tea for two and two minds are better than one, a refresher course is in order

True physical work is a necessity for getting any thing of the spirit done: may I help you more, that is have this quiet acceptance of your love trickling through the universe. I can't help speaking of the stars when I do most of my dreaming at night, most of my sitting here trying not to think too much, aware of the stars overhead, above the roof sailing. I am tired of the useless dying of energy when I'm denying that others can love as well as I. It flows back into me. When I stop fighting fly-swatting everything debating every instance of the air I breathe, fighting off love, angry at every turn, irritable at left or right, turning into an abscessed vegetable unable to move I move out up away rototill all around trying to find the cover to the septic tank and then walking everywhere looking for cut fruit tree wood to carry it up to the house to burn slowly in the living room stove and thus heat a little bit my work room. Out of this comes the fabric of the stars overhead. The humming that is everywhere the renewed energy the changing of the attitude, the lifting of the spirits, the electricity of the mind dance, as friends and love of marriage are involved, takes me take me with you, stream of life, as my defenses are penetrated by the love I let in. What I bring to something fills the cup of what I take away. I take away nothing now. I give only this insistence of a visit with the gods, the God of one and only one and all. The Gemini constellation sails over overhead. As the friendship in it commands attention: open your eyes it tells me, open your eyes to the showering of the gold or is it pollen wheat flour dust, the sunlight that isn't now

creates serenity settles as this
through as down well instant.
the they in as What
window say my the was
rainbows maybe heart, body, it
on they in the you
the know our body said?
wall a heart of I'll
of peace of my always
my that hearts, spaced be
mind. goes the out here
Work beyond solitary love for
hard any mind becomes you:
peace under- is real enjoy
and standing loved as life.

I DON'T KNOW SPANISH

I write this so someone may pick it up
and have a laugh.
Then I will love
giving them a laugh
they never could have had
without the silly have-to's and turns
of my writing.
I don't give a damn about
anything serious
because all that is is
self-pity,
or something so terrible
you can't do anything about
no matter how strong
or spiritual you are
and if you're talking Spanish
and you laugh
just tell me what was so funny.
I watch Channel 41 sometimes
and I catch an occasional word.

All I can do is
admire the beautiful women
and an occasional man.
Life is like watching Spanish TV for me –
hardly ever do I get it.
But there's a helluva lot to look at.

MOIST ITALIANS

Moist Italians.
Moist Germans.
Influenza buzzards.
Whatever you do
     the French did it first.
   That's not true.
  Have *you* ever been avant-garde?
 Then how would you know?
I wish someone hadn't told me
they don't bathe but use lots of perfume.
Or was that the English.
Under those wigs.
Oh, there were moist Czechoslovakians too
Moist Bosnians
Very moist bathers
who are presently in the water.
I'm not moist
but I'm wet.
 I just put on some cologne.
  Made in the UK.
    Can you imagine an unclean
    Englishman?
     Is an English lady an Englishman?
     Is a donut a cigar?
      Why have you come here –
       to express your dance sequences?
I can't follow the X's on the floor
because I don't have my glasses.
Oh there were moist ancient Egyptians
but they've dried up now.

IN THE MEDIA CONQUISTADORS RULE

In the media Conquistadors rule
in their quest to colonize the poor
fueled by the screeching self interests
of the Lords and the Kings and
    the Queens supporting them.

Go out and sicken the disenfranchised
starve them, incarcerate them
get them off the streets.
Isolate your self from them
while charging them high rates
and starvation pay in service jobs.

The Conquistadores of finesse
poison the public with pills
and lock children out of good schools
deny anyone wealth but themselves.

The Conquistadors of finance
suck public money out to
fuel their jets
eliminate the public services
and build up their impenetrable walls.

The Conquistadores of the sport of the wealthy
your hubris turns you into Don Quixote
as your emblazoned eyes die in pitiful bathos
the anti-climax of your fame is in
the Earth's name.
And let her name be the word
the Queen, Queen of Earth
of gigantic Spring, rises maiden-like always,
from your permanent death.

TAKE ME UP

The gizmos of God operate in the clouds –
oh profound delight, in seizures, don't come to me
    unless you mean meaning.
I'm locked on to security, as a matter of fashion,
security of my own heart and nothing else, except disease.
I stayed in the Hotel Montezuma a couple nights
and heard someone playing the cello from another room.*
I'll remember it with heart-rending pleasure like a lot of things.
God's gizmos in the clouds clank and sway.
Why can't poets get together and talk without jealousy?
Why am I jealous of God, why am I so removed?
Grace of love, eat me up, am I even palatable?
Skies delight in a good feast. Humility is meaning.
I'm tired of being separate. I am digested.

  *Stravinsky, "Serenata" from *Suite Italienne* for cello and piano

CREATOR

Creator
creatoressimo
createe
creatanimee
creatimimano
creatimimana
creatama
creatateetee
creatamaso
creatamapaso
creatamapasoneemee
cre-ought
cre-eat
cre-oat
cre-ocka
creatooter
creatoter
creatot

create dot
create torah
create tear
cree ought toe
cree otter
cree ock caughter
cree ote cocka
create a cocko
create a cocka poo poo
create a cunta cuckoo
create toss a
create a teeny
create a ta tore
create a tore
create ore
crea*t*or
creator.

FOUND IN ROSWELL
(hold up Artifact from outer space)

Oh spirit, rising dance, take over
taking me with you, where shall we land
if we ever do?
We may crash, an indentation in the soil.
You have nothing to fear from the likes of us –
full of curiosity and love, if we have been true
we will be to you too
as we meet fact to face
    you from another planet
me from another place.
But I fear you may have met up with
the suspicious and the fearful,
rather than honest fellows.
Let the truth out now, always
let the truth out
may the truth be told
listen and pass on what actually happened.
What did you see? What did you do?
Gosh here is an Artifact
    the only one worth finding
may it come to light
    in all agencies in all governments
to all dignitaries in all departments
in all media, in all writing in
all doings of the corporate giants
in all secret avenues, the sun shines.
This is the Artifact I find worth finding –
what is freely given to me
I pass on.
Here it is, shiny, curious.
Detailed, genuinely amazing.
As all true things are.   /22Nov Roswell, NM

ORION MORE

The magic of Orion's belt felt so good.
He is my hero in the skies in disguise.

HEAVENLY BLESSED
Thanksgiving

Oh heavenly blessed Earth kissed
when the embrace of love is steady,
it is the rule of Paradise.
Oh right here on Earth the enlightened fall
and pick themselves up again
to be one of us and examples.
Writing and teachings lift the Spirit
a right community supports
and the highest of all powers
energizes our atoms
    and excites the Universe.
Oh community, fellowship, the band
    of each to each
as a perfect circle, touches tolerance and love.
May this Thanksgiving last
    in substance and sustenance.
Creator, created, creating
we love you through one another.
As the Earth supports the fruitful
if we cherish it, its gardeners
    and gatherers, and dissolves most greed.
Oh heavenly blessed, Earth kissed.

DANCE

Laughs suggested we cry.
Sobs suggested we laugh.
I went back and forth
and did the dance.

WALTER BECKWITH

Your sharp looks
your careful wit
your flute music
caught up by the stars.

BABY BRAIN

I give up. There is no heart left
    in the hearts left.
Wars tear everything apart. Is this "God's will?"
The machine is set and grinds on and on
reduplicating itself on the way to the bombings.
The media jazzes it up.
Old commanders are paid to come out
    and talk about tactics.
Somehow we can laser-cut the "bad" out.
"We want business to prosper the rich
and those couple-a-bad guys just obstinately
stand in our way."
That's what *they* say.   *(put on Fool's Cap)*
"Eliminate the world of 'evil'
by doing the same thing to them
that they have done to others,
except worse, much worse.
Be the big secret they were.
Don't tell anybody
and go in there and bomb the hell out of everybody –
spray those chemicals too
nobody has to know.
Kill for corporate interests to pro*gress*.
Do what you wish
It'll take years for anybody to figure out
what you really do today
here in your high chair.
Oh Holy little baby brain, highchair God,
I am your Fool but I don't know nothin'.
And being the fool I am, who cares?
Oh Baby Brain in the high chair, lead on.
The Earth's your victim, who cares.
Who knows. Who speaks.
Who dares to question.
Let's move ahead
till those who stand in the way are dead.
Oh-Oh. Oh.
    Now are you fed?"   *(take Fool's cap off)*

TOP OF THE LIST
(a Poetorial)

How can I possibly be grateful
sitting here in this body.
Well I'm breathing, for one.
And I know how to write and read.
I can see, that's Four.
Hear. Five.
Feel. Six.
Taste. Seven.
Get up and put a log on the fire.
To be able to do things, that's Eight.
And I don't have to act like some
    vengeful jerk all the time,
that's Nine.
I have a cord of wood to help
keep us warm, and we can
pay our utility bills:
that's Ten.
And all these things we have, clothes,
electronic equipment, computers
on and on, the car, the truck, my God
this house
isn't that a few dozen
a few hundred, maybe a thousand
and more
on my list to be thankful for?
And the love of my wife
my son
my family.
The dog, even
the cat.
But mostly
the Spirit of Energy that
    keeps me going –
it comes from friends, community
    and Nature, this Earth
this night.
Everything spreads out endless
like a desert landscape
full of surprises.
Grateful for feeling grateful.

DEMOCRATIC JOY

What influences the lover of life to deepen deepen
and not extend the grip of death to all
as is done now by our Commander-in-Chief, indeed
beating the drums of war to a deafening posture
some dimwit from Texas confusedly elected President
is not my Commander, my Commander
    is the God of Love
some egotistical pip-squeak from Texas
is not my Chief, my Chief is
    the Grace of Love
the Spirit of Independence
the Patriot dance of the pioneering spirit
my Grandmother and Grandfather
    moving to New Mexico with
 their two kids
    in a wagon all the way from Kansas
to farm and teach school
    and build with curiosity
a family and a voting community
wherever they were, following
the Church of their Spirit
and not following any popular demand
without questioning.
When the drums of war for some personal vendetta
    beat, beat
for the little martinet at the helm
who thinks he doesn't have to explain his actions
the ego the hubris of all vain leaders
floats to his brain like ghosts   of the past
hell-bent on blind sighted power
eliminating the opposition
and heading down the path of power and the wealthy.
This is an anti-Nature god, a dictatorial tactic
to beat us all into destruction
and ignite what's left of peace
into war of the spirit
and death of the planet.
We need a new era of Openness   and not closure.
Secrecy only leads to misdirection.

Oh questioners question
and Democracy lift your spirit to resist this megalomania,
we each one expressing ourselves
could be a new beginning as we must always begin
in freshness amazing all with our delight in Nature
our connections with building Community
and giving a hand to help up
the sick and poorer.
I only have myself to react to this evil bombing will
and I don't think it's enough.

What the bloody hell are we doing
what is my country 'tis of thee.
Are the wealthy and their gated communities
the goal of every American?
What about the rest of us.
Who is our real Commander
if not within the Spirit of Love?
Who is our true Chief if not the benefactor of the Earth
and singer of the stars?
The mystics and saints of love
the peaceful resistence that changes countries in India and America
and now the world.
Lead us oh true leader
to vote our way out of this misery.
Bring us to understanding of those in other places other countries
other behaviors, other daily problems.
May we become friends through discussion and dialogue
endless dialog
and eliminate blame from the arsenal of our vocabulary.
May we weaken retaliation by
not retaliating,
listen, listen, listen without vengeance
until the talker is talked out
and there is a silence that
the Grace of Love fills.
Let that be my leader, the deepest listening of all
where our spirits join
in democratic joy.
The pioneering spirit of democratic joy.   /4dec

SURPRISE

That's all I can do is be beautiful for you. Beautiful for me. Beautiful for the two of us. Beautiful for the lace of life, the lay of developments, the way things go, the turning of the page to what upbeat surprises:

Surprise I'm dawn. Surprise I'm the way you look tonight. Surprise I'm the moon out with the sun. Surprise I'm everything you ever wished for and more. I'm the surprise turned in slept over to awake startled – I'm sober no headache no misgivings of the past, no guilt just a breathe easy day to fall off the century of noise and enter the paradise of every myth known to man and ahoy woman. Moving textures make a plain where rain entered, green forage for over grazing cattle but surprise – a bunch of antelope all still stand out on this prairie, these plains from Vaughan to Roswell and back. Antelope and there were sheep as well as cattle.

Antelope
run
through
my
memory
as
in
my
late
dream
this
morning.
Oh
where
am
I
in
any
interruption
"I
got
all
the
tomato
poles
out
and
stacked
the
tomato
plants
in
a
pile
so
the
garden
is
basically
cleared
on
this

early
December
day
surprise.
It's
such
a
beautiful
day
why
go
into
town."
Stay
here
I
say
and
time
will
take
care
of
itself
as
well
as
space
as
well
as
the
love
woven
out
of
it
all
because
that's
what
I

can
do –
keep
my
lungs
clear
wake
up
in
the
morning
knowing
what
I
did
last
night
and
be
beautiful
as
this
sunny
day
clear
as
a
message
out
of
the
blue –
me
you
me
you.
Be
beautiful
out
of
the
blue.

What
is
this
all
about
and
why
go
there
smiling.
Why
not
go
there
smiling
as
long
as
you
don't
over
do
it.
Smile
like
a
merchant
marine
coming
into
port,
not
like
that
minister
on
TV
whose
smile
never
leaves
his

lips crack course. it
but a Of into
that's smile course consideration
what you I'm in
this dodo. not fact
is I'm smiling I'll
all speaking now do
about. to but it
Why myself I'll now.
not of take Thanks.

WIDE OPEN

It's opening
   up openings   all of
     up openings   us getting
       up it's   hungry in
         to go   my imagination
           outdoors with   we are
            company   following and
             dream   following
              a   each
             dinner   other
              party   this
               go   is
               out   my
              with   dream
             them   dreamed
              out   with my
           of the   eyes wide
          house out   open.
        is opening   See.
      nature opens
    up to
   you to
me to

GONDALAY

This happened: Gondalay came to me and said,
"What good are your yarns?
You tell them and tell them but don't tell them to others.
Your hands hold the secret of tomorrow.
Share them today.
Go tell anybody who will listen."
And then Gondalay went away.
I was left here wondering who he was
who he is?
Someone who is concerned about me and what I do,
that I'm not doing justice to myself, to what I say.
Thank you, Spirit Friend.
I'll get out of my shell and do what you say.
I need you in every way.

RENEWABLE ENERGY

The time, tied up in knots, began to wobble.
Space, getting old, began to crack.
Matter, all matter, slowed down and shrank a little.
Then everything heaved a gigantic anthropomorphic sigh.
And then, over time and space and matter, the sigh
turned into a breath. There was universal breathing
slowly *in,* everywhere was aware of it
even outside of the big bang where everything slept.
Nothing itself, at the very center of the galaxies,
was breathing in, and then through aging,
it all, in, filled to capacity, began to release itself,
absolutely everything turning around and
whirling, spiriting, breezing out, all things that mattered
in time and space slowly refreshingly breathing out, out.

VOICE PRESENT

"Never do
I go
far away
from you
Earthling lover
but you
abandon me
every day.

Shall I
make myself
visible now?
As if
I haven't
always been
in front
of you,
in back
of you,
surrounding
you
to each
side of
you,
above
below and
in the
very center
of you,
as I
live and
breathe now.

In your
innermost self
alone with
you we
are a
living twosome.

Do I
make myself
clear, am
I visible
now, all
around and
in you?
Stretching beyond
you in
your friends
too, and
your wife
your son
the granddaughter
every one?

Am I
visible enough
now oh
Earthling lover?
Do I
need you?
Yes, you
say, I
need you
to pray.
That love
comes naturally
from you
as you
pray to
me I
am you
and move
beyond
ourselves
as more
and more
is revealed.

Pray to
me every
day,
especially
in the
morning,
love
the morning
light and
love creates
wisdom as
day falls
neatly away
into night.

Say to
me any
time of
day or
night what
ever direct
thinking thing
you say,
in love
I need
from you
so we
can build
together from
my will
for your
creative good
so you
can enjoy
the helping
hand you
give to
others, I
need you
to help
me with
them too.
Am I
truly visible
am I
making sense?

Are we
in living
partnership
together
in this?
Let's keep
together and
others will
love us
as we
love them.
As I
speak to
you through
them too
when we
meet together.
And speak
one voice
at a
time who
can say
which one
is mine?
No matter
what, we
have power
together, I
am nothing
without you
you can
say to
me, as
I, yes
to you."

THE ETERNAL MUSE IS NOT ARROGANT

The Eternal Muse
is not arrogant
is not prejudiced,
guides, does not demand
builds, does not destroy
gives gods words
on what to do.
Enters the songs of poets
the words of music
notes of a time when
Earth surprises.
There is a no time better than
night
rising out of the ocean
or the simplest pleasure
or any day
between moments
when two words adjoin
into a phrase that floats
into consciousness.
It is everywhere
to those open to
its odd moments,
the between times
when out of a crevice of a rock
a flower grows.

So to speak
how to thank the openness
open to her opening
his hand
the joining of my brain tool
and that vista.
To give thanks is
ultimately to be open
turning the ego back
which throws everything
off course
so what can grow
from where,
something that has to do
with peace
in all ways
coming out in song
those great songs that
resurface
if I give thanks
by not standing
in the way.

THE ETERNAL MUSE DOES NOT KILL YOU

The Eternal Muse
does not kill you
with values
you cannot use.
It comes from the pain of love
breaking

when to feel deeply
penetrates energies
yet unknown.
The explorer
exploring in his own way
what untraveled
what unmarked by human
touch
pops out
around every new corner.
Out of love
life loving life
comes.
In cities
in this village
wherever dreams
rise to the surface
in sleep.
And the logs in the stove
are burning –
this December is
a value
of twelve months
the deepest.
The deepest energy
which may not come back
with the sun.
Especially now
it's difficult
to find a new orchid
there's no jungle here
but I can
explore
and find
the value
of listening.
Listen while you can
you man of dreams
everything bubbles up
from the woman of love
as we rise to the surface
together
hand on my dreams
I can't remember.
Heart beats
still
I hear the dog scratching
the floor
with his paw
dreaming.
They're talking about Big Foot
on the radio,
big brain, big heart
where do they find it
big finger
big lips
big eye
big liver
big belly button.
Oh he was found
at the center of the Earth.
She was doing a dance around
or was it she
who was found.
Big She
Big She presence
the heart of hearts
at the center of the center.
We have to be cared for
whether we care for it or not,
she said, obviously,
fresh as dawn.
We have dominion over nothing
but our self-destruction.
Good is the good,
evil is living the lie.
There is only value in this
obviously
this dawn,
this fresh light.

༃

POETRY LITE

Is poetry so mysterious you can't get a handle on it?
Is it a pot a kettle a pan a mug?
Is it a valise, a suitcase, an appliance
a door prize, a soup.
Is it a tedious catalog you'll never order from?
Is it under your thumb?
Can you put your finger on it?
Is it only Dante? Is it only Whitman?
Is it only Gertrude Stein?
Is it oblivion in flight.
Is it whatever comes into your headless torso?
Is it an incredibly beautiful lover you can never touch?
Is it an academic exercise to get you a job?
Can you pin it down?
Can you hit its nail on its head?
Is poetry constipation? Something you have to
    strain and grunt to get out?
What language is it in?
If I speak Gargantuan and you speak Minutia
    is there really any translation?
Can poetry be translated at all, except by a poet?
Do poets have handles but poetry does not?
Does poetry have to have an audience?
Is that its handle?
Or is the poet the audience's handle?
If poetry doesn't have a handle, does it have a crutch?
And is that crutch the poet?
Or is poetry the poet's crutch?
Where is the mystery?
Who killed that bad fly?
Is this poetry lite?
This is poetry lite.
You have to purchase and download the heavy stuff.
My whole life has been lite, except for the heavy stuff.
If you want to know the truth I never could afford it
because I wasn't willing to work for it.
Therefore lite.

Lite is spelled l-i-t-e and light is spelled l-i-g-h-t
because lite is lite light.
Lite light, that's the handle, the pizzazz
the pith, the marrow, the substance, the secret ingredient
the mystery of it, the inordinate essence
the inestimable value, the power, the glory and the goal.
The process of light enters the darkness and as we go
    zooming through synapses
the miraculous treatment occurs. One with the singing.
That singing I hear, I'm one with it, or is it
ringing in my ears. My ear, wow.
Those are the handles.

HOLE

The Spirit moves me though I don't understand.
    What is the Spirit?
Is it a knockout of God.
    I thought knockouts were thrown away.
These are pure gold.
    Should I go find one for myself.
That's up to you.
    Do you have one?
No.
    Then what do you have?
I have the hole it was knocked out of.
Is that enough?
More than enough.
What does it allow you to do?
Love you.
    What do you mean?
Love me, but only as a vessel
    where things can pass through,
like the hole.
You mean this little circle of emptiness
    is of value to you?
It's an endless circle and all things can pass through.

COMPOST

Everything continues as the amazing African gazania
    exotic animals whirling around in space
plants of another dimension communicating healing arts.
Birds bash into satellite towers until they fall
    and the birds, half dazed, continue on their way.
Migrating fools go to Washington and are ripped off
    by corporate darling prostitutes who work
        for the CIA and deal drugs from Bolivia.
North and South kiss in the middle of the Earth and plan
    to exchange places and save the planet.
Coming up to the mirror the most beautiful porno babe of all
    meets the most beautiful guy of all
    and they can't see each other as they walk away.
Spirits move in the darkness and become ghosts, shadow people
    angels, UFO aliens, Big Foot, monster of the deep,
        demons and scattered paraphernalia of the gone mind.
Paranoia King hosts breakfast for school children
    as they jump up and down with glee eating
        their monster soup but are afraid to go home.
The mish-mash God supports every interpretation
    of war-hungry executives and rolls back
        the stone on Jesus, incarcerates Buddha
            castrates Mohammad and poisons Coyote.
Finally the great Whirl of Space energizes resistance
    and evolved seeds throw off their genetic upstarts.
        The forests begin to grow through tractors.
            Bombs defuse themselves.
                Young men discover their beautiful sensitive graces.
Women take over finances and put their domestic houses
        in order.
    Human population begins to go way down
        fewer and fewer and fewer
until the planet is manageable, that is, the planet manages.
Stars stellar sing, night's skies bring romantic breezes.
    You don't have to have children to be of service
        to the sick and dying.
Oh what a revelation, the skies sing.
Earth has gardens again.

DOORS

Oh Light, light the path
on the least light day of the year.
 Be with us in the darkness, light light
 the showering way, the opening dawn of clarity
 as doors open doors, hand hung doors
  front doors, back door, portal doors
   doors to help each other
   out of traps, out of traps of mind and body
   out of dark holes into less dark ways into
   a turning where tolerance is an act
    where love is a play
    where the day is growing into the day
     and honesty is a dramatic scene
      the end of the play
       as the lights come on
        all the way. /21Dec Winter Solstice in memory of Andre

TINKERER

Nothing seems right.
Everything seems optional to what I should be doing.
No matter where I am it doesn't seem right
unless I tinker with something.
I lie down and the curtains are closed and I can't see
    the dawn coming on.
I sit down to read and there's no reading lamp,
    just the overhead lamp.
I'm always tweaking, adjusting
getting up to change something,
trying to control the atmosphere.

AN EVEN DOZEN

An even dozen, what is it?
Golly bum is it eggs?
Disciples? Inches in a foot?
Why is there no word for a group of eleven
    or thirteen?
There's a couple, for two, or more.
And then there's a half a dozen .
Then there's the dozen, an even dozen
what's an uneven dozen?
Then you jump all the way to a hundred
And then a million.
Of course there's half-a-million.
And a quarter million.
That would be nice, dollars of course.
At least a dollar is a hundred cents.
Makes sense.
I'm glad there's a dozen of anything really.
The 12 steps.
The Olympiad, the Greek Gods.
The Zodiac.

BACK DOWN

I need to come back down to Earth
and read some Creeley poems.
My head has been in the clouds
of unknowing.

What actual things are
is
and not what my mind
casts on them
or would have them be.

Back to back with particulars.
I'm sitting on the "throne"
addressing the world.

THE TROOT

Poetry is no longer alive.
It's at the dead center of things
keeping everything else alive
mysteriously.

ON THE TIP OF THE TONGUE

Give me what is with the blessing –
    you are behind it
as Power takes the form of love
    in many guises.
See as you may, do as you see
your tongue lifts me to the sunlight.
As ever the unknown leads the known
broadcast out from you,
gives me the strength to be grateful
in need of giving
as it fills me to overflowing
    in your many forms
    grows without whining
open to dawn making, love enlightening. /25Dec

ORGOPOOPIA.

The first stage of consciousness is the Orgopoopia.
In the Orgopoopia I can find my lost wits.
Gather your wits about you for to die witless
    staring at the blank is no good.
We died 3 times before we lived once
and entered Orgopoopia.

ALIEN CLASSIFIED

❖   I was taken up by a gosling who squashed my tomato and gave me love therapy. Ever since then when I hear the word L-O-V-E I seize up in my boots and can't move for ten minutes.

❖   Hello my name is Charlie. I'm from Alarid, Texas. When the passion came over me I took all my clothes off in the forest and I saw a clear light and ascended for ninety-two days although when I got back it wasn't more than two. These little pink and buff creatures lay me on a massage table under a blue light and that's all I remember for day after day. There was hovering around and all my pores got sucked by little mouths. When I got back there was no forest and my clothes were dirty and there was only this that I'm telling you.
Are you scared?
Yeah, every time I look out the window I get a bleep.

❖   Now my story is different. They swept me off my feet and gave me a prom dress and there was a ball in that big round saucer and we danced all night. Every once in awhile they came at me with it looked like knitting needles and kind of poked away at me. They were all shorter than me and I'm 5 foot 2. I danced so much, when they deposited me back home in my bed I was sore for days. This is all I think about.

❖   They come and get me over and over. All I have to do is close my eyes and become part of things. It gives me a nose bleed some times. It's that old black magic. I don't see voodoo dolls when they take me away, they *are* voodoo dolls and they're trying to turn me into one of them.

❖   Hi my name is Chuck Tamale and I'm from Northern Lackadaisical, Florida. You know they were little green creatures and they performed an operation on me. They made me quack like a duck and then waddle around the table before they'd let me go.

✧   They were very kind and very fair. My name is Harriet. They only want to find out about us. Before I went to sleep they said don't worry. Their speech was kind of broken and then I had a strange dream where I was back on Earth being normal again. They even thanked me when I woke up. For what, I asked. "Don't worry" they said. "What we replaced in you should last longer than you do." I've had a physical. There's nothing wrong with me except every once in awhile my eyes turn purple.

✧   You know I'm a skeptic. I thought this was all BS. Then one night I had a terrible fright I put up a fight but they got a grip on me tight. And I ascended up to a height and they did things to me under a green and yellow light. And when I got back I've never been the same. I walk out naked in the rain. I don't know who to blame. I have a little fame. And I have some apprentices I train.

✧   Hello I've never been anyplace. Do you think they'd be interested in me? In any of my organs? Is there a classified section for those who want to be abducted? I've got an interesting belly button. Do you think if I paid them they'd take me away? How do you get a hold of them. Do you just wait? What kind of cologne should I wear?

✧   Hello my name is Suzie. This is serious. It's a matter of life and death. I've never been the same since I saw that light and I was transferred inside some how. It was awful what they did to me. I've been in hypnosis sessions and it keeps getting uglier and uglier.
   Like what?
   Well they lay back a flap of skin though it didn't hurt too much. It was downright unpleasant. They were kind of mean. But I couldn't move. That place on my breast still itches. And then they did something to my shoulder and that still pings every once in awhile. I can't go out at night anymore. All I do is watch the prescription ads on TV and wonder if there is anything to help me. At least I'm not the only one. But I feel terribly alone.

✧   Hello I'm Dick from Albany. I don't believe any of this. But at the hour of ten every night these big bug eyes come in at me. And they take me away in this giant bug and don't bring me back till after midnight. I don't believe any of this but there are these big bug eyes. What shall I do? I'm terribly blue. Big bug eyes have got me all in a stew.

~∂

MINIMUM WAGES

What do ants make an hour?
What is the daily wage of a rhinoceros?
How much do birds get?
Those bees, do they get paid overtime?

PERMISSION TO BE TRUE

Are there honesty wagons in the heart of life,
little children pulling them into adulthood?
What a delight, the true spirit, unhampered.
Is there any left in me, if there ever was, where is it?
It takes exercise of the body, a simplification of the soul
to be a part of that child again, in me,
that can form me every day into the privilege
of wide open skies, a dream of knowing
I can be open too, if I let it flow.
Oh flow little spirit, the plaything of the heart
is the seed of truth, as I was a young gardener
carting shit in that wagon for some use.
It is now, through work only, the perfect flower
that breathes through me, every day, if I let it be. /31Dec

DIAGRAM OF LOVE

Who would be interested in
a diagram of our love for each other?
Here it is, anyway:

Two lost souls
found each other
inadvertently
gold.

༄

Breath
End

NOTES

Note: p. 5 *et al I* "free free free in the sober state of reality...." I'd been sober 5 years in 2000.

Note: p. 172 I consulted Kenkyusha Japanese Dictionary which said "Contracted" "Minor sentence" "John!/ Look here!" and since my new notebook was small I wrote short lines, only one word per line or two in several poems.

Note: p. 181 Beckwith was fellow student in the Roswell High School marching band.

Note: Do-It-Yourselfers: William Blake, Lord Byron, Thoreau, William Morris, Stephen Crane, e.e. cummings, T.S. Eliot, Robert Bly, Robinson Jeffers, Rod McKuen, Poe, Pope, Shelley, Tennyson, Whitman, Sandburg, Pound, Gertrude Stein and thousands more recently.

BREATH

alphabetical

A Big Meeting 152	Cliche Exploded.............. 92
A Bit of Peace................. 80	Closer 101
A Body Discovered 161	Cloud of Knowing 28
A Flow...................... 17	Coloratura Bossa Nova 151
A Gentleman Beggar.......... 163	Coming Out of It............ 157
A Japanese Sensibility......... 125	Comments 204
A Lesson in Listening 43	Companion 119
A Pastoral 145	Compost..................... 192
A Piece of Your Peace of Mind... 51	Confession Confusion......... .98
A Perspective................ 127	Connected 129
A Piece 2	Coolest 36
After Suns................... 55	Creation Plus 114
After Sunset 20	Creator 175
Alien Classified 196	Crushing Ego Wars 57
All I Have 46	Dance Slowly 93
American Portrait 116	Dance of the Atmosphere....... 22
An Even Dozen 194	Dance 177
And We Thought Gertrude Stein 79	Dancing in Now We Trust 24
Anthrax Avenue............... 78	Death Spurt 120
Are You a Bodhisattva?......... 68	Democratic Joy 180
Ass First Through the Cosmos.. 149	Diagram of Love 199
At Last 92	Die Oh Log.................. 148
Baby Brain 178	Discourse While Eating 67
Back Down................... 194	Doors 193
Bad Day 110	Down the Drain, A Holy Book... 74
Bats........................ 127	Drama of the Heart........... 126
Beast in Man 42	Drug 67
Between Us Sings 58	Duo-Mono 19
Bowl 43	Duties...................... 27
Breath...................... iv	Earth Love 37
Breath, Feather, Fresh Air 87	Easter Sunday 2000........... 18
Breath 2002................. 95	Eating the Light 156
Breathe Easier 13	El Malpais................... 84
Breeze Speaks 62	Emptiness is Not Enough....... 84
Brilliant End................. 108	Enjoy Life 10
Budding 6	Enlightenment Is the Patootie.. 160
Bury the Lie 26	Entranced................... 52
Busy Going Noplace 30	Eons Speak.................. 167
Cartoon..................... 158	Epithalamium 140
Charm...................... 109	Eulalia Hope 102

Exotic Enchantress	69	In Medias Res	101
Face In My Food	56	In Your Service	22
Fall (Oh Cabezon)	75	In the Media Conquistadors	174
Fall Morning Glory	164	In the Calm	112
Feminine Ending	142	In My Jungle Home	89
Fighting Big Egos To the End	131	In The Stars	168
First Breath	122	In One Place	107
First	118	Index	201
Fish Story	105	Intensity Too	14
Flow	34	Interrelation	117
Flower Again	55	Is It True?	89
Flower	40	Is Isis Isis	120
For My Closest	119	Jazz Set Me Free	121
For the Cowboy Buddha	146	July Twenty Second	141
Found In Roswell	176	Just A Piece of Peace	6
Freely	47	Just Friends	132
from Heartbeat	35	Just The Best	25
from The Direction of One	88	Just Is	114
G.O.D.	130	Just For Fun	149
Gift Giving	155	Ken	1
Glad	128	Last Play	86
Gondalay	185	Let Out	32
Good	134	Lighter Times Will Flow	17
Good Day	110	Limbo Dust	134
Goodbye	75	Listening, for Delon	15
Greater Than Reality	135	Listening Love	61
Guide	100	Literal	117
Hairnet	111	Living in the Problem	81
Hands	129	Loneliness Lit Up	.97
Happiness is a Thrill	64	Lonely	93
Head Over Heels	54	Love Appears	67
Heavenly Blue	71	Love Evolve	167
Heavenly Blessed	177	Lubriderm	165
Helping Our House Be Nice	9	Making Up Places	147
Her Cue	116	Meditations	156
History of the West	29	Mind	41
Hole	191	Minimum Wages	31
Hum Joy	163	Minimum Wages	198
Hummingbirds	158	Moist Italians	173
I Don't Know Spanish	172	Mood Elevators of the Dharma	48
I Shot Clarity	94	Moon Jump	37
I Am Nature	64	Moon Haiku	159
Image Nation	162	Mormon	76
In the Middle of the Night	3	Morning After Thanksgiving	92
In Secrecy	42	Morning Tea	70

Move Over	23	Result of Meditation	93
Move Over	12	Riddle	86
Mutual	122	Right Now Alien	130
My Ego	154	Right On	121
My Mind Is A Garbage Truck	25	Robber	126
My Piece of Flying Saucer	138	Root Level	144
New Breath	72	Roswell North	166
No Strings Attached	116	Sad Story	104
No Mystery	46	Sam Schwartz	40
Note from Gary Brower	v	Screw Loose Logic	165
Notes	200	Seeing Drink	128
Now A Muse	161	Servants of the Earth	30
Oh When I Die	75	Shock Talk	108
Oh Cabezon 2001	35	Simplicity	139
On The Tip of the Tongue	195	Sloth	7
On the Way	132	Sloth Kill	36
One On One	123	Smaller Worlds	3
Open To	37	Sober Bartender	85
Open Ancestors	8	Solar Heat	77
Orgopoopia	195	Sold For Profit	124
Orion More	176	Some Call It Grace	149
Out of Itself	11	Something Was Inspiring	115
Outside-Inside	33	Song	12
Over Pop Stranglehold	63	*Spring* (Oh Cabezon)	42
Parked in the Garage	4	Stampede of Morons	155
Partners Return	159	Stand By the Source	2
Path	21	Stars, Lead Me	23
Permission to be True	198	Start Off	90
Plantation of Real	48	Steps	100
Play the Game	7	Sublime Teacher	13
Poetry Lite	190	Such As It Is	.96
Powerless and Free	83	*Summer* (Oh Cabezon)	64
Practice	85	Sunlight Light	45
Praise	8	Surprise	182
Pray, That Is To Say	123	Take Me Up	175
Prayeritis	35	Talk	109
Pre-Dawn Dance	109	Tell Me	49
Precious Wisdom	61	The Eternal Muse Does Not Kill	188
Preface	v	The Greatest Story on Earth	106
Quote	106	The Truth of it All	44
Reality Note	164	The Happy Poultry Club	50
Recent Books	205	**The Light No Stars 2000**	1
Red Dust	95	The Joy of Rejecting	53
Relax Into Me	134	The Troot	195
Renewable Energy	185	The Earth and The Heavens	16

The Well of Turquoise. 38	Unchained Melody 82
The Magic Knob. 9	Unconscious Sonnet 99
The Wood. 133	Under Stars. 150
The Round Robin of Love 145	Up From Sleep 12
The Last Party on Earth. 31	Visitation 11
The Eternal Muse Not Arrogant. 188	Voice Present 186
The Art of Life 79	Waiting At BCDC. 41
Thinking Straight. 111	Walter Beckwith 177
Tinkerer 193	War and Peace 148
Tiny Tinies 44	We're Innocent 117
To the Old Pope. 117	Wet Body 42
Top of the List 179	What Ever Happened to Fine. . . . 63
Touched 60	What the Heck. 118
Tough Turkey. 143	What Is It 166
Towards Sunset 11th of July 21	Whole 160
Troubled 6	Wide Open 184
True Self 41	Wild Hungarians 50
True Love 76	**Winter** (Oh Cabezon) 35
Turning My Back 137	Wishful Stinking 148
Two Parts of the Same Thing 7	With One Heart (To Song) 136

Joy Harjo: "Poetry isn't the property of Academe. It's an *alive* art – and you [lg] prove that."

Jimmy Santiago Baca: "He experiments with form, he charges the poems with incantations and chants, his tone shimmery heat rising off the text, or ecstatically sparking small fairies fire-flying off his shoulders – Placitas guru dancing in the dust of your garden, whispering that resinous piñon aroma in your love verse, poking fun at the breakfast cereal box portraits of presidents and their crackling hypocrisy . . . ."

Gus Blaisdell: "Goodell is a *natural,* a category that academe either explicitly denies, actively discourages, or has forgotten." - from "Co[s]mic Clown," in *Artspace*, Fall, 1976.

Photo Lenore Goodell

RECENT BOOKS

Escape - poems 2003-2007; *Grounded* - 2008-2010 poems
Commons - 2017-2019 poems
duende press 2020
Hot Art and Other Plays; *A New Land and Other Writings* (prose)
duende press 2019
Nothing To Laugh About - 2015-2016 poems
Beatlick Press 2018
Pieces of Heart - 2014 poems; *Digital Remains* - 2013 poems
Broken Garden & The Unsaid Sings - 2011-2012 poems
Beatlick Press 2015

3 dimensional poetry   https://larrygoodell.blogspot.com/
lotsa larry goodell   https://larrygoodell.wordpress.com/
duende.bandcamp.com for recordings / @larrygoodell

The Larry Goodell / Duende Archive is at the Beinecke Rare Book & Manuscript Library. "It is a unique record of the thriving poetry and small press cultures of the Southwest (and New Mexico in particular)."
Steve Clay, Granary Books
cover photography and design by lenore goodell
larrynewmex@gmail.com   larrygoodell.com

DUENDE PRESS
the original   established in 1964
placitas, new mexico usa

www.ingramcontent.com/pod-product-compliance
Lightning Source LLC
Chambersburg PA
CBHW020852090426
42736CB00008B/347